G. L. Tottenham

Harry Egerton

Or, The younger Son of the Day - Vol. III

G. L. Tottenham

Harry Egerton
Or, The younger Son of the Day - Vol. III

ISBN/EAN: 9783337122751

Printed in Europe, USA, Canada, Australia, Japan

Cover: Foto ©ninafisch / pixelio.de

More available books at **www.hansebooks.com**

HARRY EGERTON;

OR,

THE YOUNGER SON OF THE DAY.

BY

G. L. TOTTENHAM,

AUTHOR OF "CHARLIE VILLARS AT CAMBRIDGE."

"Non equidem hoc studeo, pullatis ut mihi nugis
Pagina turgescat."
PERSIUS.

IN THREE VOLUMES.

VOL. III.

LONDON:
CHAPMAN AND HALL, 193, PICCADILLY.
1869.

LONDON:
PRINTED BY VIRTUE AND CO.,
CITY ROAD.

HARRY EGERTON.

CHAPTER I.

THAT wiser Satan that tempts by making rich, had selected in Harry Egerton a good subject for the practice of his wiles. This *coup* of two or three hundred pounds had produced exactly the effect desired.

Exalted by continual and increased good luck, he began to think that he was marked out for especial favour by the fickle deity who presides over money speculations, and, accordingly, the amount of his stakes was proportionately raised in future.

The immediate result, however, was a sumptuous dinner to his friends, where the prospects of the Two Thousand, Derby, and future meetings were discussed with confident anticipation of success; where much generous liquor was also discussed; and where dull care, tradesmen, and all such periodical annoyances, were drowned in the flowing bowl.

Some of his debts he paid off, and a few of the more pressing of his tradesmen, with whom he thought it might be politic to settle while it was in his power so to do. A handsome wedding present was selected for Maud Greville, and everything, for a few days, was *couleur de rose*. A new era had arisen for his fortunes; a career of profitable speculation was opening out before him which might result in anything—marriage perhaps. Should he ever really be married? The thought occurred now, freshly tinted by hope, and more softly attractive, if possible, than heretofore, from having for several weeks lain by neglected; and Blanche's soft features and constant love were dwelt upon with a double rapture—produced, partly, by the nearer prospect of enjoying them, and partly by a consciousness of their having been thrown rather into the background of late by the excitement of betting, and the engrossing occupation of making future calculations.

This, at all events, was something to work for,—a worthy end for his exertions. And don't jump to the conclusion that he could not have cared much about her if he allowed his mind to be so entirely occupied with excitement of another kind. It was some time since they had met. He had tried to give up thinking of what was not to be; and betting is the most effective distraction to the thoughts. There are such innumerable combinations, and complications, and changes, and surprises, and calculations, and possibilities, and re-arrangements, and anticipations, to occupy the mind, that there is very little room for any other subject—even love; and that, supposing it to be nurtured by far less disadvantageous circumstances than Harry's was. A hero of romance ought, you think, to rank love superior to any other enjoyment or excitement; but he was not so much a hero of romance as a younger son of the period,—and that, I daresay, is the reason why he acts here in such a very unusual and unnatural manner.

Be that as it may, there was very little doubt that at the present time his spirits were very high—so high that Spencer Greville, meeting him in St. James's Street one afternoon, supposed that he had made it up with his father, and congratulated him accordingly.

"Not a bit of it, my dear fellow," Harry rejoined, gaily. "He's still on strike, with every prospect of remaining so. But I've been making money on the turf lately, so that I'm more or less independent of his humours. Won nearly three hundred a few days ago!"

"Then I should recommend you to stop before you lose it all again," returned Greville.

Lose! Ha! ha! what a good joke! "I haven't any intention of losing, my dear Spencer," he said; "I'm going to win a pot of money on the Two Thousand and Derby, —the last particularly." For on this race he had some bets which he said were worth hundreds to him even now.

"Take my advice, and stop before it's too late, Harry, my boy; you'll come to grief if you don't, depend upon it! You can't always win, you know, and no gentleman ever does win in the long run at betting."

"Well, I've done pretty well this year, at all events," Harry said, rather annoyed that any doubt should be suggested of his not having the game all his own way.

Greville, seeing that his advice was as distasteful as such advice always is, did not press it any further, and Harry turned the conversation, a moment after, by asking what he had come over to London for.

To make some arrangements about Maud's settlements had been Greville's primary object.

"You know, of course, that she is to be married at the end of the month?"

"Yes, I know," Harry replied. "They were in town a few days not long ago. I saw them then, — not for long, though.

Philip came in when I was there (in my father's house I mean), and as good as told me to leave the premises."

"Nonsense!"

"Fact. Oh! he's a very pleasant fellow to have for a brother. We are *so* fond of each other!"

"By the way, that reminds me," Greville said, after looking incredulously at him for a moment, "when I was turning over a lot of old papers the other day, to look for a deed that bore upon these settlements, I found a letter from your father, dated about the time of his marriage, a sort of formal acknowledgment it seemed, promising that your mother's fortune should be settled on the younger children of the marriage, if there were any. I never heard of any such settlement having been made."

"It has not been made. I asked old Bond about it in the winter. I was rather hard-up at the time, and thought I might have raised some money on it."

"I thought it was very possible that it might have been done without my knowing anything about it, for of course it doesn't concern me in any way. But it ought to be done. Your father's life is not a particularly good one. He might die any day, and you would have no security for the payment of the money. This letter would only be useful in so far as it would show what his intentions were. Philip, I suppose, would act upon them, but still——"

"I'm not so sure of that," interrupted Egerton. "I'd sooner have it on paper. But of course I couldn't suggest it: don't you think you might?"

"I hardly know. I never was very intimate with my uncle, and he's not the sort of man to suggest advice to. I should think he would probably do just the contrary to what one suggested."

That was quite possible, Harry said. "You might, at all events, let me have this letter," he continued; "it might come in useful some day."

Of course he was welcome to it, Greville said. He was the only interested party.

"I suppose, in a legal point of view, it

is no use?" Harry said, as if with a purpose beneath the question.

"None, I should think. You couldn't raise money on it, if that's what you mean; at least I shouldn't think any money-lender would consider it security even for a hundred-per-cent. transaction."

"That's a bore! but anyhow send it to me when you go back, will you?"

Greville promised that he would. "But you had better come over," he said, "and stay with me for Punchestown; you have never been there."

Harry hesitated. He should like it of all things. But unfortunately the Newmarket First Spring Meeting clashed with Punchestown, and to miss that, he said, would be so much money thrown away. He promised to think about it, and let him know.

"By the way," he continued, "there was another thing I wanted to ask you about. You never told me anything more about that old mad woman at Castle Greville. Are you there now? I suppose not. In Kildare?"

"I'm only in Galway in the autumn. But really I had nothing further to tell you," Greville said, smiling: "except that she seemed very grateful to you (as they always are) for some money you had given her one day. Said that the Lord would reward you when you came into your own, and indulged in many other equally vague expressions."

"Well, for choice I think I should prefer something down," Harry said, laughing. "I think I could be induced to compound for any prospective reward. All that I can call 'my own' at present is a couple of very neat parcels of bills, of which no one seems inclined to relieve me."

"But seriously," he continued, changing his tone, "there may be something more in what she says after all."

Greville smiled, and was about to rally him on his mystery. But Harry proceeded to tell him of his aunt's strange conduct the last time he saw her, of Philip's chance hints too, which all pointed in the direction of some secret connected with himself or his birth, and which had haunted him ever since.

It was not pleasant, all of a sudden to have a doubt thrown upon his origin; and he had felt so fully convinced, from his aunt's half-admissions and his brother's insinuations, that there was something to be found out, that he had determined to find it out come what might.

As a first step in that direction, he had gone to see Lady Belvedere a few days after, and had questioned her upon the subject; but she had looked at him in surprise, had never heard of anything of the kind, and could throw no light upon his foreign sojourn which would tend in any way to help him. Still Harry could not get out of his head—he knew it was very foolish, but there it would stick—he could not help recurring to that conversation where Lord Staunton had said that there was something unexplained about the death of Lady Belvedere's son. "What could that have to do with him?" he argued. "Supposing that they had been the same age,— what of that?" And it was likely enough that these Jesuit fellows Lord Staunton had talked about had a purpose to serve in getting rid of the child,—if they did,—which he had never heard, except from Lord Staunton, to have been the case. Mrs. Greville evidently knew more than she cared to tell; and Philip,—there, again,—Philip, too, knew something about it. What object could he have for concealing it? It couldn't be love for him. Perhaps he didn't know anything for certain, perhaps he had only picked up hints dropped by Mrs. Greville, perhaps what he knew was to Harry's advantage, and therefore kept back. Then there was this old mad-woman in Ireland. If she could only be made to talk sensibly, something might be got out of her; but Greville treated the thing as a joke, and probably had not tried seriously to draw her. He did, however, confess that there was something strange about the various circumstances which Harry recounted to him, and said that the old woman had talked very queerly when he mentioned his name, or Philip's, or any of the family; but then, she always did talk queerly, and he really had not taken much notice of what she said, so that there was not much satisfaction to be got out of him.

But Harry was not the less fixed in his determination to get to the bottom of it somehow, although he couldn't see his way beyond the surface. However it turned out, he could not be in a much worse position than he was at present. Perhaps that was the reason why Mrs. Greville was shy about telling him what it was she hinted at,—motives of kindness,—not wish to distress him. But then his father?—it was a puzzle, and as unsatisfactory as all puzzles are which are difficult to make out. So he continued to brood over it at intervals, and try all sorts of conjectures, which led to equally hypothetical solutions. And unless a kind Providence provides some unexpected means, it seems improbable that he will ever get beyond the state of perplexity in which we now leave him.

CHAPTER II.

FINDING that most of his sporting friends were going over to Punchestown, Egerton decided to give his victims in the ring at Newmarket a temporary respite, and availed himself instead of Greville's hospitable offer. Expense was beneath his consideration at present, so that it mattered very little whether his trip to Ireland cost him one sovereign or twenty. As he had gone over there to enjoy himself, it would have been folly to allow any such absurd reflection to intrude upon his mind, and therefore no such reflection was allowed to behave in this offensive manner.

L'homme propose, and he had intended to have returned to England braced up for the season, and ready to encounter whole armies of book-makers under cover of his armour of luck. But the event grievously disappointed his anticipations. He found that it was quite as possible to lose money in Ireland as to win in England, and that there were quite as many betting men willing to lay the odds at Punchestown as there were at Newmarket. He lost on nearly every race. And, growing desperate towards the end of the last day, left off a loser of far more than he had won on the Grand National.

He found his intended regiment too, quartered at Newbridge; stayed with them a night; played cards; and at the end of the evening there were several names down in his book for sums which there seemed very little probability of their ever receiving, unless his luck recovered itself again in England.

His visit to Ireland had been an unmistakeable failure. He had broken in upon his run of luck. He had had his military longings revived by seeing what a jovial good set of fellows they were amongst whom he was to have been quartered. His would-be military feelings had been irritated over his losses by many a dirty old woman's " Ah! captain, dear, won't you buy a box of matches?" or the intensified humour of " Major, darling, won't you throw the poor old woman a copper?" He had been sold by a little vulgar boy with newspapers, whom he had asked, during the agony of some bitterly facetious spasm, for to-morrow's paper,—receiving for reply that it had been disposed of on the previous day. He had almost had a row with a dyspeptic Frenchman in the cabin of the steamer, for digging an umbrella into his (the Frenchman's) side, as he lay in the berth above and poured out the long-drawn sweetness of a foreign snore. And he had missed the opportunity of adding to his fortune at Newmarket—where, as he found on looking over the week's racing, he must have won on nearly every race. He should have backed this horse, and this, and this,—all winners,— and he had not backed one of them! Never was such bad luck! However it couldn't be helped now. He must only make up for it at future meetings. And with this good intent he arrived again in London. Greville accompanied him on his return, bringing his little girl [with him to officiate in the capacity of bridesmaid to the future Lady Farringford.

The longed-for day arrived. The sun shone out upon the white favours of the carriages which had attracted a small crowd about the door of St. Paul's, Knight's-bridge,—a bright atmosphere, smart dresses, cheerful faces—all the elements of a gay and happy wedding were there. And Harry felt very small as he elbowed his way through the bystanders, and sneaked quietly into a back pew, where he would not be seen. He had half a mind to go out again, and cut the whole concern. But then he fancied that Maud might think it unkind of him, as she had made a point of his coming. So he stayed, and tried to amuse himself in watching the group in the chancel, amongst whom he ought to have been himself.

How painfully shy and uncomfortable

the unfortunate bridegroom did look as he tried to make conversation to the people round him. Poor wretch! his mouth was dried up with nervousness. And how very much out of place Philip's disagreeable features seemed in the midst of that gay company! Harry believed he had come there intentionally to mar the effect. Then he passed on to Lady Belvedere's magnificent attire, the bevy of would-be brides, and Mrs. Greville's already tearful face. What a life she would lead, he thought, with his father, when Maud was gone! And after lingering a moment upon little Constance Greville's bright face, he began to think that weddings were very poor fun to look on at—why on earth had all these people collected?—when a buzz of expectation proclaimed that the carriage which had just rattled up to the door contained the bride. And very charming and fresh and pretty she looked in her Brussels lace and orange flowers, as she walked blushing up the aisle, leaning on Mr. Egerton's arm.

Harry's eyes pass quickly on from her to

his father, whom he has not seen since they parted so many months before; and involuntarily he feels the tears rising in his heart, as he notes that his step is less firm, his figure less upright, and his face more careworn than it was last year. These few months have made him an altered man. He no longer holds his head up with the haughty, independent indifference of former days. There has been a gnawing worm at work, undermining that careless enjoyment of life which his face was wont to express. Harry feels that it is all his doing, reproaches himself as the cause, and longs to throw himself at his father's feet and tell him so. What wouldn't he give at this moment to bring back the easy, happy expression to which he had been accustomed? But then the thought arose that his hands were tied, that his father had been himself the destroyer of his own peace, that he was powerless to remedy it—the door was shut against him, and anything he might say or do would only be attributed to mercenary motives. And he tried to steel his heart against any feelings of love or compassion by assuring it that he had been ill-used and hardly treated, and that if his father wanted him to come back he had only to say so: the remedy lay in his own hands. He had made it impossible for him to contribute in any way to the happiness of his life; and so he really didn't see what he had to be sorry for. But nevertheless, while the service proceeded, his eyes would wander every now and then to the point where his father stood, and rest upon his bending form with a look of affection which his resentful reasoning was not strong enough to repress.

The ceremony is over, the conventional tears have been shed, the bride and bridegroom feel intensely relieved, and a move is made towards the vestry.

Harry, to avoid recognition by any of the bridal party, leaves the church at once, and is a subject for interesting speculation to the attendant footmen as he passes through them out into the crowd. With scarcely a glance at the line of carriages which were going to convey the honoured guests to breakfast at his father's house, he saunters on moodily towards the park.

And why should he now be sauntering on moodily towards the park? and why should his father's bent and altered form be exciting the commiseration of such of his friends as have not seen him since the previous season? Isn't it because Mr. Egerton is deliberately creating additional misery for himself and his son (over and above the ordinary share allotted to mortals) out of the very circumstances and relations which should most have contributed to their happiness? Isn't it because he is now experiencing that selfishness—for parents may be selfish to their children just as much as any one human being to another—must always have the effect of turning into a mere sunless existence the bright panorama of human life, where the shadows are only meant to set off the recurring sunshine?

"Nous retrouvons dans nos enfants une seconde jeunesse," says Madame de Staël, " dont l'espérance recommence pour nous quand la première s'évanouit." But how often does one see parents living their lives over again in their children? Is it a common sight to see an old man forgetting his age in the enjoyment of life which he is able to provide for young people? Isn't old Martin Chuzzlewit a much more usual type of character than Colonel Newcome? Are there many men in the world who have found out that the real happiness of having money lies in the means which it affords of making others happy; that living for the pleasure of others is the surest way of making life really enjoyable for themselves? If Mr. Egerton had had a spendthrift son, for whom he had already done more almost than it was his duty to do—whom he had been obliged at last, out of justice to the remaining members of his family, to give up in despair—such a son as his namesake, who has already figured in these pages—we should then pity the old man's heart, wrung with a yearning affection for his prodigal son; we should take off our hats to the grief which was bowing him down in his old age. But in the present case, we really must positively refuse to see any occasion for the exercise of compassion other than towards the son who was anxious to reform, and was not allowed to do so. Let Mr. Egerton forego the selfish gratification of his love of consistency; let him learn to acknowledge that the son has a claim to consideration equally with the parent; and then we may congratulate him upon awakening to a better condition of mind, and heartily wish him all the happiness which doing his duty is likely to produce.

But Harry is already in the park, and the morning world is there also. The Easter recess is over; London is returning or returned. The budding leaves are looking fresh and green, and the early captain in full bloom.

Cowper, I think it is, who says that a man must be a great friend indeed for you to receive a slap on the back from him without your friendship being endangered. How, I wonder, would he have received a smart tap from a thickish cane by way of greeting from a man who was nothing more than an acquaintance?

Egerton, perhaps, was never less disposed to receive without irritation such an unwarrantable familiarity; and his good-humour was not increased when, on turning round, he was accosted by Captain Mullins, with all the easy freedom of an old acquaintance and friend.

"How are you, Egerton, old fellah?"—almost patronisingly it was said. "Come to town for the season—eh?"

Harry replied, with the most frigid civility, that he was well—thank you.

"How's the old lady—eh?" continued his friend.

"What old lady do you mean?" asked Egerton, who may have conjectured that Lady Belvedere was the person indicated. But he was unwilling to afford any facilities for conversation.

"Why, the old gal we were staying with in the country, of course," returned the other.

"If you mean Lady Belvedere, my aunt, I believe she is very well."

"I say," Captain Mullins then continued,

in a confidential tone, taking Harry's arm at the same time; "how about that heiress? Is it good enough?" And Captain Mullins grinned a jocular grin beneath that bushy moustache, and looked knowingly at his brother captain, who hung upon the other arm.

"What heiress?" Egerton asked, innocently. "I really don't know what you mean. Would you mind explaining?"

The position in which he found himself, walking up Rotten Row in company with a brace of unmistakable captains, was enough to make anyone a little short in temper.

"Oh! of course not—sly dog!" replied Captain Mullins, and he again broke into a guffaw, and poked Egerton in the ribs with the end of his cane. Captain Mullins, you see, was a bit of a wag.

Harry said he was sorry not to be able to see the joke, and the Captain went on to inquire whether there were many swells in town.

"Only came up that morning," he said,

as if it was strange that he should have delayed so long in the country. " Cremorne open yet?"

"I really couldn't say," Egerton answered. "As I hardly ever go there, I don't take much interest in their proceedings."

All this while he was torturing his mind for some excuse to escape from the monstrous presence, which was doing such violence to his self-respect. And yet he must have been very particular; for the young subalterns of Captain Mullins's regiment were only too proud to be seen in " the Row" under his wing. Such a well-dressed man! Such patent leather shoes, just showing a glimpse of a gaudy sock! Such a silver-headed cane to loll upon the railings with, and suck! Such a smart cut-away coat, with scarcely any tails, and trousers fitting like a glove! And the spotless yellow gloves must not be neglected, or the scarf of brilliant hue, and hat of curly brim. Oh! it was a distinguished appearance!—and he knew it too, did this gay dog of a captain.

But, somehow or other, Egerton didn't

seem to know it. Or perhaps he wouldn't know it. Perhaps he thought that his own quiet, black frock-coat, and other articles of dress which were not in the height of the fashion, might appear to small advantage in company with such a beau as Mullins. That must have been it—he was jealous. The Captain, however, was not at all so anxious to part company; and he next proceeded to attract Harry's attention to the various female celebrities as they cantered past; the remarks of himself and his friend upon these interesting subjects being so edifying and instructive, that it is not without a certain compunction that they have been omitted, in deference, perhaps, to the wishes of the British public, who rather object to being edified.

It was quite touching, too, to hear Captain Mullins reproach Harry with his faithlessness in not having been to see him at his barracks, as he had promised. It was quite sad that a growing friendship should be so soon nipped in the bud.

Egerton made some very slight excuse,

and almost forcibly unlinking his arm at last, said that he couldn't possibly stay any longer—engaged to lunch.

"See you in the Burlington this afternoon?" asked Mullins. "You do the Burlington, I suppose? It's the thing to do in the afternoon."

"Is it?" said Harry, drily. It was rather amusing to be told by a captain what was the thing to do in London. "I'm afraid I shall not be there. Good-bye."

Captain Mullins's military friend observed, as Egerton moved off, that his friend's friend seemed a very haw—damme kind of chap. Where did Mullins pick him up?

The captain with the whiskers hereupon gave a detailed account of his stay at Belvedere in the winter (most of his friends knew that he had been to Belvedere), and was good enough to say that Egerton was one of the right sort, not half as stuck-up as most of these young London chaps.

And so they continued to loll and to stare and to ogle, and to ape the ease of regular frequenters of the place until the ride became deserted, and they gat them away to their Rag to discuss the events of the morning over their cold beef and ale; then had a turn at billiards, perhaps, until it was time to air themselves in the Burlington Arcade, and make eyes at the women in the shops, and stare and leer at every petticoat that passed. From thence to "do" the park again in the evening.

CHAPTER III.

A FEW days after Maud's marriage, the papers which busy themselves with such intelligence announced the arrival of Mr. and Lady Mary Villars and family at their mansion in Grosvenor Square, for the season.

The announcement caused the heart of one individual, at all events, who read it, to beat some degrees quicker. We need not disguise from our readers that that individual was Henry Egerton. "Odd!" he thought. "Why had Charlie not been to see him? Should he go and call? Of course he must; it would be only civil." And the thought of seeing her again, of being now in the same town with her, of running the chance of meeting her any moment in the streets, caused quite a flutter of excitement in the young man's breast; and then he thought that Lady Mary would probably just as soon that he didn't go—but Blanche! Ah! he didn't think it would be the same with her. But how could he tell? It was months since he had been at Mottistone: she might have forgotten him. In the country she was—delicious recollection!—but London was a very different thing—people were never the same in London. Perhaps he had better wait till he met her somewhere, and then he could pretend to have only just found out that they were in town. That might be a long time, though, he considered, ruefully; and the next day he had persuaded himself that, after staying with them and all, it would be exceedingly uncivil not to go and call. Besides, he wanted to ask after his friend, he wanted to know where Charlie was, why he hadn't been to see him; and the day after, he had determined that it was his duty to call at once. There is clearly a kernel of truth in the shell of cynicism which encloses Rochefoucauld's dictum that our passions are the only orators that invariably persuade us.

In pursuance of his resolution, upon the propriety of which he no longer entertained a shadow of doubt, Harry finds himself on Sunday afternoon standing at the door of the family mansion in Grosvenor Square. I don't mind telling you that he was a little nervous and excited, and that his hand had shaken a little as he brought down the knocker with a rather feeble summons. True, it was out of regard for his friend's family more particularly that he had called; but how would Blanche receive him? She was in there now—only a wall between them. Why didn't they answer the bell? The second since he had rung. seemed to have been an hour.

Blanche heard his knock, but continued reading, in fluttering unconsciousness, until the drawing-room door was opened, and Mr. Egerton announced. Then she dropped her book with a start, which was very gratifying to her visitor, and blushed a bright rosy red, which was also gratifying to observe, as she advanced to meet him, and told the servant to let her mother know that Mr. Egerton was there.

He rather wished that she had omitted this order; but that intelligent servant, who had seen him at Mottistone often enough, and knew pretty well the state of affairs between Mr. Henry Egerton and his young mistress, kindly deferred making the communication as long as he thought he could prudently do so; and they were, therefore, left to themselves for several very pleasant minutes.

Her mother was tired, Blanche said, and had gone to lie down. Blanche had been under the impression that no visitors were to be admitted. She said this in an arch kind of way, as if to reproach Harry for being there with her now; but she didn't mean it, and he knew that she didn't.

He was not quite at his ease, however, just at present, although he tried very hard to appear as if he was; and he said something about hoping that he had not disturbed her.

Of course, Blanche was not going to say

that he had. And she looked at him, and he seemed to find so much in that look that he actually—yes, really, he felt that his face was quite flushed with a tingling sensation which that look occasioned. It was a pleasant sensation. She had not changed in the least, he told himself; and they understood each other perfectly during that momentary silence while Harry flipped little grains of dust from his hat, and Blanche settled the lace upon her dress to her further satisfaction.

Had they been long in town? he asked.

Not long. They had seen him two or three days before walking in Piccadilly, but Blanche supposed that he had not noticed them.

How she had been thinking, and waiting, and expecting, and wondering whether he would come, and starting at every ring at the bell, ever since, no one, of course, but herself, knew.

Under the sedative influence of commonplaces, the embarrassment natural to a meeting after a long separation gradually wore

off, and Harry then asks after her brother,
—supposes that he didn't come up with
them, or that he should have seen him
before now.

"Oh, didn't he tell you?" Blanche answered. "He's canvassing for Mr. Grey,—
our neighbour, you know. I should think
you must have known him at Cambridge;
he was there with Charlie."

Oh yes, Harry knew him very well. He
had heard that Grey was standing for some
place in the country, but he didn't know
that it was near Mottistone.

It was not near Mottistone, Blanche said;
but her father had property there, and
wanted Mr. Grey to get in, so Charlie had
gone to help him. He had been there some
time,—nearly a fortnight.

"I didn't know what he was doing,"
Harry said; "he hasn't written to me for a
long time. He isn't a good correspondent."

"He's very lazy about writing. I don't
think he ever would write if I didn't look
after him."

"I ought to be very much obliged,"

then," said Harry, looking as if he was very much so indeed.

"But I didn't mean about writing to you only, Mr. Egerton," rejoined Blanche, in some confusion. "I meant to everybody."

"Still I have something to be grateful for, even if I only come in for a share."

Blanche does not immediately reply; fiddles with her handkerchief, and there is another pause.

"You never came to see us again, as you promised," she said, without looking up.

"No,—I'm afraid I didn't keep my promise; but the fact was—I could hardly—I mean I had so many other engagements" (what a glaring fiction! when he had been cursing the dulness of the winter in London). "I was staying somewhere else when Charlie asked me to go, and ever since I've been——"

"I'm afraid you've been gambling," interrupted Blanche, with a confidence which showed that his movements had not been without interest to her. "Charlie told me that you had been going to races a good deal. And as you talked of doing something reckless last year, I thought that—that you might be losing more money."

And although he assured her that he had not done so, the possibility of it seemed to cause her some uneasiness, for she went on, a little shyly at first, to remonstrate with him on the risk which he ran; and then grew quite earnest about it, until it flashed upon her that she was showing too great an interest, perhaps, in his proceedings.

He, however, didn't think so at all. It was not by any means unpleasant,—very far from it,—being lectured by her. And he really felt very meek and happy under the infliction, as he looked occasionally into her face, and found it animated with such a lively interest for himself.

"But what is one to do?" he asked, very humbly.

"Oh, there must be many other things to do besides betting," Blanche said; "and gamblers always come to some horrible end."

The prospect seemed to have occupied her

thoughts before, for a slightly pained expression passed across her face as she paused.

"I'll give it up at once," Harry said, impulsively, "if you think I ought to. But when one is winning there can't be much harm, can there?"

"But you can't always be sure of winning, I suppose?"

"I'm afraid you think me a great ruffian, Miss Villars; but it really isn't my fault."

"No, indeed, I don't," exclaimed Blanche, warmly. "But I do wish you would give up betting. I'm sure you'll be sorry some day, if you don't." And there was a tinge of melancholy in her voice, Harry thought, as she said it.

"Well, after the Derby, I'll promise not to bet any more," he said, after another pause.

"But I have no right to make you promise," Blanche said, colouring again, and saying that they had known him so long that she had said a good deal more, perhaps, than she ought to have. But Charlie would be so very sorry, and all that; and you might have seen, from the nervous movement of her foot, that she was a little embarrassed how to find an excuse for having said so much.

Lady Mary's entrance fortunately created a diversion, and although she saw with some concern that she had interrupted what seemed to have been a dangerously interesting conversation, her manner to Harry was not a whit less cordial than it always was.

They had the talk now pretty much to themselves. Blanche said very little, but seemed to be thinking a good deal; and you might have seen her eyes stealing over towards Harry, when she thought he was occupied with her mother, and not looking her way. And then, if he moved ever so slightly, down again they went to the ground, as if they had never moved from there the whole time. And once they were intercepted; and though Harry betrayed no outward sign of gratification, his next remark was sadly confused and uninteresting.

Lady Mary had been going over the same ground as her daughter, and telling him all about Charlie; and he had got up a fresh interest for all the intelligence which he had just been hearing respecting the prospects of the election.

He was staying with a Cambridge friend, Lady Mary went on to say—a Mr. Rowley, who was a curate in a neighbouring parish. Did Harry know him perchance?

Oh yes, he knew him very well—was he staying with him? He had met him last year in Norfolk. He was in London then.

Lady Mary believed that he had only lately gone to his present quarters; but Charlie seemed very comfortable, and——

Her remarks were here interrupted by the opening of the door, and the entrance of the Marquis of Galston. He preferred generally to give his title in full to the servant.

The easy assurance and *habitué* of the house air with which he strolled into the room rather astonished Egerton's unprepared mind. And when his lordship gave him a slight nod, as much as to say, "I don't mind your being here," and then turned to address himself to Blanche, as if she was his confidential property, his surprise turned into a most considerable aversion. "What the deuce does he mean by his impudence?" was the idea which was uppermost just then in his mind; and had my lord Galston been conveniently situated for the purpose with regard to him, I haven't a doubt but what he would have gone down the stairs a great deal quicker than he came up them.

Lady Mary bore up bravely under the difficulty of the situation, and tried to keep up a conversation with Egerton, while Galston was endeavouring to make his platitudes palatable to her daughter. But Harry had less inclination now than ever for talking, and his answers and remarks became hopelessly absent and pre-occupied. It was some little satisfaction to him to hear that Blanche was treating Galston to a coldness, and almost haughtiness of manner, which he had never observed in her before. The fact was, she had been annoyed more than once by his assumption of a claim upon her attention. In the present company such a manner was peculiarly irritating; and Galston therefore made but little way in her affections this afternoon. But since even his happy unconsciousness of adverse opinion was not proof against a series of almost monosyllabic answers, he began at last to find out that he was not getting on quite so well as he flattered himself that he usually did. Other girls were generally so glad to talk to him, that they took upon themselves the burden of the conversation.

So he turned to Lady Mary, and shared his valuable ideas with her. And Harry, finding that he could no longer sit in the room with him (he had at first determined to see him out), rose to go, shook hands with Blanche (jealously watched by Galston), said good-bye to Lady Mary, and, taking no notice of his lordship, left the house, full of the most benevolent and happy feelings generally,—but, in particular, entertaining most charitable and kindly views in regard to the noble lord whom he had left behind.

He ultimately determined that, should circumstances favour the carrying out of his present humane designs in respect of that person, he would be showing a really Christian-like and self-denying moderation if he were to abstain from indulging his desire to *hit* his lordship, and were merely to soothe and relieve his agitated feelings by sitting upon his head.

The idea, I have reason to believe, was adopted from a suggestion thrown out in a recent number of a weekly publication called *Punch*.

CHAPTER IV.

It was evening in the early days of May. The same sun which stretched its level rays across the deserted heath at Newmarket, which dazzled the eyes of home-returning undergraduates, and shed its golden beams upon unappreciating groups of noisy racing men,—this same sun was lighting up a very different scene in a quiet country parish far away. The undulating landscape was decked with all the freshest tints of spring. Spring was in the atmosphere, in the meadows, in the hedgerows, —everywhere. Primrose and violet peeped from every mossy nook. Honeysuckle and sweet-briar scented the evening air. The rich green of the meadows mingled with the darker woodland hues, and light balmy airs, laden with the perfume of woodside flowers, came rustling through the trees, and sighed themselves away amid the shining ivy leaves, where little birds were twittering their lullaby to hairy little fledglings. There was over all that calm and beautiful repose, that quiet sense of peace and pure enjoyment, which is peculiar to the soft evening-time of spring.

Villars and Rowley stood at their cottage window enjoying the scene, until the last rim of the declining sun disappeared below the line, and twilight began to steal upon the darkening woods—adjourning then to the dining-room, and their simple meal.

Rowley had only but a month or two ago exchanged the dirt and distress of London for these country quarters; and being not dependent upon his eighty or ninety pounds a-year stipend, he had taken unto himself this comparatively luxurious cottage.

What with his trellis-work and twining roses,—his comfortably-furnished dining-room and sitting-room,—his flower-garden, bounded by ivy-covered wall,—his rustic chairs,—and his vegetable garden, with the early peas already in full blossom, it was an enviable little retreat for one who cared little for the so-called pleasures of society, and the noise and tumult of the world,—who wooed that "passionless bride, divine Tranquillity." Pictures and books kept old associations in remembrance; a spare bed-room accommodated a chance friend; and occasional cricket with the village boys recalled sweet memories of early triumphs —while the respect of his parishioners, the confidence of his rector, and the satisfaction of feeling that he was doing his duty in the world, all added to the charms of this simple life, which contrasted so attractively with the scenes of misery which he had so lately quitted.

It is the evening before Villars' return to London. The election is over, Grey has come in, and his labours are at end.

They have been talking over the excitement of the past few days, and Charlie is congratulating himself that all his dirty work is over.

"Canvassing," Rowley replies, "always appears to me such an undignified proceeding; going round to people and fawning upon them, and pretending to take such an interest in them, just to get them to vote for you."

"Well, it is, rather," Villars admits. "They like to show their power over you. They don't get the chance, you know, very often. A man told me the other day that a fellow promised him his vote once, and then spat into his hand, and held it out by way of clenching the business, 'There's my hand upon it.' Of course he had to take it, or he wouldn't have got the vote."

"I'd have let him keep his vote," Rowley said. "If I ever stood for a place, I should just tell the electors my opinions and principles, and then, if they liked them, they might elect me, and if they didn't, why I suppose they'd elect somebody else."

"You'd stand a very poor chance of getting in anywhere in that independent kind of way."

"But if everyone were to do the same,

they'd have to elect somebody, and then the best man would probably win. It ought to be the electors who want to be represented, not the representative who is eager to be elected."

"I suppose it ought really; a little on both sides, perhaps. But who's to begin? It sounds very plausible; but there are lots of men who have a position to make, and plenty of money to spend, who would do anything to get into Parliament. Your independent gentlemen would soon go to the wall when these fellows were canvassing all the electors, and we should have a money Parliament."

"Well, I'm not a statesman, so I don't pretend to say how it is to be obviated. But it's very odd if some Act couldn't be passed to equalise everybody at starting. I'm all for making the constituencies pay the expenses of the candidate. It would give poorer men a chance. And I think the way elections are conducted now is almost enough to keep any man of any self-respect from trying to get into Parliament."

Villars didn't see his way to Rowley's Utopia, and, accordingly, they adjourned shortly after to Rowley's garden.

"Why didn't you come here at first?" Charlie asked.

"Because I didn't know anything about the work," he answered; "and I thought it would be a good thing to take a winter in London, just to get into training."

"What work? Is there anything to learn?"

"Schools and visiting, and all that sort of thing. And one requires to get accustomed to the kind of life, and giving up amusements, and other things of the sort."

"It must have been a fearful life, though, wasn't it? I think it was very praiseworthy of you to go in for it," Villars said.

"I don't think that," Rowley answered, quietly. "There are only too few there as it is. No one who hasn't seen it can conceive the amount of distress that exists. And people will persist in increasing it by giving to beggars in the streets, actually putting a premium upon pauperism. If they would only give their charity through recognised societies, there are quite enough deserving cases to absorb it all."

A pause, and then Villars asks, "Have you given up cricket, then, altogether?"

"Almost," he answered. It was hard to forswear his pet pursuit, but he had done it.

"But surely there's nothing wrong in playing cricket, is there?"

"Nothing whatever that I can see; but if you are playing cricket all day you won't have much time to attend to your parish work; and then, even if you had time to play, people would always say that you thought of nothing but amusement, and didn't care about your duty. So that it's just as well not to give them the chance of saying it; then they can't lose their respect for you."

"Of course you wouldn't ever hunt, then?"

No, he wouldn't. Not that he thought it wrong in itself; and what was not wrong for one man was not wrong for another;

the same rules of morality applied to all alike.

"But then," he continued, "I think that hunting isn't a sufficiently sober amusement for a clergyman to indulge in without insulting the gravity of his profession; and so many people are scandalised at the idea of a hunting parson, and think he must be a godless sort of man, not fit to administer the sacrament, that it's better to avoid bringing one's office into disrepute by doing what would have that effect, even though it may be harmless in itself. I don't think there's any objection to a man's hunting, out of his own parish, when he's away for a holiday; where his own people couldn't be offended at the sight of his boots and breeches."

"I suppose it's very wicked to say so," Villars continued, presently; "but I don't think I could have gone into the Church; there would have been so many things one would have had to give up."

"I don't know that it's particularly wicked," Rowley rejoined; "a little ignoble, perhaps. Everyone was not born to be a clergyman, and there are many other lines of life in which you may be equally useful, where prejudice will not oblige you to give up harmless pleasures. Of course, if your life is to be useful, you can't afford, any more than we can, to devote the greater part of your time to amusement."

Villars did not reply, and they continued to smoke on in silence for some minutes. Perhaps he was wondering whether he ever did do anything but amuse himself; whether Rowley's self-sacrifice in the cause of duty might not be a nobler kind of life than the indolent existence which he was leading. The idea of duty, perhaps, had never occurred to him before—probably it seldom does to young fellows situated in his position, as eldest sons and heirs to a life of ease and empty waste of time.

Rowley's thoughts, meanwhile, had wandered back to those haunts of wretchedness amidst which he had spent the tedious winter months, and had recalled from the gloomy past the sad scenes which he had witnessed, the melancholy tales which he had listened to, and the heart-rending cases of distress which he had been unable to relieve. And, among others, memory had called up before his view the emaciated, neglected figure of that man in the lonely garret, who had a name of high repute, and birth equal to his own, and who now seemed to reproach him with forgetfulness of the assistance and interest which he had promised to exercise in his behalf. "How stupid of me!" he exclaims—as he wonders how the case could have slipped thus easily from his memory. True, there were many others with an equal claim; and he had shortly after changed his district. Anyhow, though it was rather late now—for the man might be dead—here was a chance in Villars. He might communicate with his Cambridge namesake.

And Rowley, therefore, proceeds to detail to him the particulars, and promises to give him the address when they go indoors, in case it may be possible still to find the man there, and to do something for him.

"You know Egerton's address, I suppose," he continued—" what is he doing now?"

In London, Charlie believed, at that moment, or, more probably (and this conjecture was the more correct of the two), at Newmarket. "I'm afraid he isn't doing much good. His father refused to pay his debts for him, and turned him out of the house; and the consequence is he's going rather to the bad."

"He lived rather expensively at Cambridge, didn't he?"

"Not nearly as much so as a great many other fellows. I had a good many bills when I left, too; but my father paid them all for me, and only told me not to get into debt again; and I haven't."

"But then you're an only son."

"He has only one other brother; and his father has plenty of money. I think it's a very hard case."

Perhaps it was, Rowley said, but he was not altogether sure about it. However, after a little further thought, he said that he should probably pay his son's debts once, if he could afford it; and then, if he got into debt again, he shouldn't pity him, if he had promised to keep clear in future, and had not kept his promise.

"At any rate," he said, "you might tell him about this man; he may know something about him. And I dare say it won't be a bad thing for him to see what it is possible to come to through gambling and extravagance."

"What a pleasant notion!" cried Charlie. "Poor old Harry! He shan't come to a garret if *I* know it." And he wondered how Blanche would like the idea.

"There's no saying where a fellow may stop, if he once begins to go down," Rowley said. "I expect these sort of stories are common enough all round us, only that they don't often come under our notice."

Rowley himself had always lived within his income, and therefore, after the manner of those persons who have not succumbed to temptation themselves, he was inclined to view Egerton's position in a rather more unfavourable light than Villars liked—in fact, he rather took the father's side, and Charlie got quite angry presently in defence of his friend.

When he went so far as to assert that, after all, he couldn't see that there was any great harm in getting into debt, Rowley gave up the argument. It was useless to attempt to argue with anyone who asserted the principle of self-indulgence. So he suggested that it was getting chilly—hadn't they better go in and have some coffee?

The other grumpily assented, and the discussion terminated.

CHAPTER V.

THE unconscious object of the conversation which brought the last chapter to a close had been far too interested in the retrospect of the day's racing and the morrow's prospects to take any note of the beauties of that calm sunset, or, indeed, to have a thought for anything at all beyond his betting-book. The tide had turned with him at Punchestown. The wheel of fortune was not always going to give up prizes for him. And he was obliged now to acknowledge that winning was no certainty. Still he continued to brave his luck—increased his stakes, and lost again. And at the end of the week's feverish excitement, he had lost enough to make him a considerably sadder, if not a wiser man. How was he to settle? This question would keep recurring to his mind as he returned to London, and it was to no purpose that he racked his brains to devise some scheme for raising the required funds. The only thing for it was to get some reckless friend to back a bill. And among his present associates such a friend was not very difficult to find. His horror of bills had by this time considerably diminished. The great thing was to get money. It mattered very little now what means were employed. So the money was got. His account was partially settled, the remainder standing over till after the Derby. And having taken the precaution to retain certain funds for present exigencies, he endeavoured to dismiss for the time his embarrassments from his mind—an endeavour by no means easy to put into practice, when every day brought him fresh letters of application from exasperated creditors.

A note from Lady Belvedere one morning, delivered in company with several missives of this objectionable kind, turned his thoughts into another channel. It asked him to dinner on some not very distant day. Miss Grant was to be there, Lady Belvedere said—and the sly old lady had placed a little note of admiration after the intelligence.

Harry had met his aunt's heiress more than once since her return to town, and had been received by her with a gracious interest which would have been most gratifying to any adventurous young man whose affections were not already engaged. But he was fresh from the sweet renewal of his love in another quarter, and had no eyes or heart at that time for the civil speeches and smiles of any amount of wealth.

Now, however, when his temporary good fortune seemed to have deserted him, and difficulties were closing in on every side, and driving him occasionally to the utmost tether of his wits to find means to meet them, Lady Belvedere's note brought up again a glimmering notion, which in spite of him would flit about his mind at times, and he fell to thinking. A good deal might be done on six thousand a-year, and more in prospect. House in London—dinners, by Jove!—box at the opera—moor in Scotland—yacht— hunting quarters in Leicestershire, and a house full of people to trot about the deer park—live like a prince, instead of like a hunted vagabond. The idea began to grow upon him—no more duns—cut the turf—become domestic—but with her—eh? And at this moment a carriage turned the corner of the street, the sight of which put to flight in a second of time all those dissolving mercenary views which had only the moment before appeared so delightfully attractive. What a thrill of remorse and disgust with himself Blanche's smile occasioned him, and what coals of fire that gentle look seemed to heap upon his head! He knew that he deserved it, too—not the look, but the punishment which it contained. "If she only knew," he thought, "what was in my mind at that moment—what a scoundrel she would have thought me! and she wouldn't have been very far wrong either." And then, as if to make amends for his former misdeeds, he indulged in all sorts of imaginary endearments, and fondled away her injured look, and made all kinds of vows and resolutions, and woke up from his pleasant dream, anathematising, for the thousandth time, his want of money.

Among other resources which in his extremity had been tried for the purpose of obtaining funds, he had made an attempt to negotiate his father's letter on the subject of his mother's fortune. But the sixty-per-cent. Israelite to whom he had applied had smiled at his innocence. The document was useless as a security. It was very possible that the gentleman who had done him the favour to call might be Mr. Egerton's second son, and, indeed, his only other son. That in itself would be an interesting question for investigation (Harry inwardly agreed with him there). But even so, at present it did not appear that the money had been settled upon him at all. If he could produce a deed to that effect, and give any reasonable proof that he was the person he professed to be, then, the usurer said, he should be happy to do business with him—very happy indeed (for he was a civil usurer)—particularly as, by referring to his papers of many years back, he found that a gentleman answering in name and description to the applicant's father had been a very good customer of his.

The knowledge of this fact gave the son no particular satisfaction, when it led to no results for himself; and he went away a trifle more despondent, perhaps, than when he entered the usurious sanctum. It was very odd, he thought, that he, a perfect stranger, would not give him credit for being his father's son. The man's suggestion had, of course, only been prompted by the caution natural to his profession—but Harry, pervaded now with the knowledge that there was some doubt hanging over his identity, could not help fancying that it had a more direct application. And he again gave himself up to wonderment and irritation against his aunt for giving him no clue. It was so aggravating, too, to know that Philip appeared to have some private grounds of suspicion which he had not been able to trace to their origin, and which it was very unlikely Philip would confide to him of his own accord.

Very unlikely indeed! for Philip hoped to derive much sweet satisfaction from working out the matter for himself. It would quite spoil the pleasure of the thing if his brother was allowed to have a hand in bringing about his own ruin. Still, that would be neat, and gratifying too. That was a happy thought! and when Philip's knowledge was a little more precise, it might be managed so. It would be pleasant to look on and watch him eagerly pursuing the mystery to its source—that source the destruction of his own position—to see him springing a mine upon himself.

With the view of putting him in the way of such a pleasing occupation, Philip had made another journey to Shoreditch. He was beginning to know the line of country now, and could save the cab fare the greater part of the way. This time, however, he had deemed it advisable to disguise his proper person, in order to court admission with greater probability of success; and he had bewigged and bedizened himself with whiskers and shabby-genteel garments in a manner which he fancied would defy recognition,—if, indeed, recognition was the point of consequence; for it was quite possible that hitherto his dress had been too good for the locality, and excited suspicion. If suspicion had been excited, the sinister aspect of his countenance had been to blame, rather than his clothes. But Philip naturally was not aware of this; so he practised his disguise before the glass till he felt quite at home in it, got his story well into his head, and sallied forth to conquer the taciturn relict of the deceased attorney.

He played his part so well upon the opening of the door, that he was actually admitted, and very soon found himself seated face to face with the little bent old man whom he believed to be the depositary of his coveted information, and whose keen scrutiny he found very difficult to undergo without betraying signs of uneasiness. The difficulty now was to lead up to the subject which had brought him there.

For a few minutes he continued to carry on the deception which had introduced him, and then, breaking away from it abruptly, he said—"But the chief reason which brought me here, Mr. ——" and he paused, as if with the expectation that the other would supply the wanting name.

But that fixed countenance gave no sign, and Philip continued—" I am not at present acquainted with your name, sir, or how far you may have been in Mr. Flint's confidence," and he paused again, but the other continued to look at him without giving the slightest encouragement or assistance; and again Philip proceeded—"But I was about to say that my chief object in coming here was to make some inquiries in the interest of a friend—a friend—whose name—is Egerton."

" Yourself."

This was the only response which came from the shrivelled lips. Since when the discovery contained in that little word had been made, Philip had no means of conjecturing; and therefore, though startled a little out of his self-possession by the suddenness of the announcement, he thought it better to make a virtue of necessity, and assuming a most charming and innocent frankness, admitted that he actually was himself; that he had been induced to disguise himself in this way, owing to his attempts to gain an entrance on two previous occasions having, for some reason best known to the old man, failed,—although, on the second occasion at least, Philip had reason to suppose that he was in that very room at the time.

His explanations seemed to evoke no shadow of interest from the person he was addressing, who continued to look at him with a perfectly expressionless face, and an imperturbable taciturnity of manner.

Philip continued: "I was anxious to know whether your late partner had communicated to you some important information which he was possessed of in regard to my family."

Still no answer.

"Whether he had taken you into his confidence in the matter of my visit to him some months ago—early in November it was—in reply to an advertisement inserted in the *Times*, to persons of the name of Egerton. He had appointed another day to see me, and unfortunately died in the interval. I thought that, perhaps, you might be able to supply the information which he desired to give."

He went on eking out his explanation, hoping at each pause that the old man would strike in, and say something, at all events; but as he showed no desire or intention of making any observation whatever, Philip at last was obliged to put it to him in the uncongenial form of a straightforward question. Did he know anything of the matter? Was it in his power to give the information which Philip sought?

And to these questions he received a monosyllabic "Yes."

"You will do so, then?"

"No."

"No!" echoed Philip; and then continued: "Of course I hardly expect you to do it for nothing; though, indeed, it concerns me but little to know what you have to tell. My brother would seem to be the more interested party; but still, as I have an interest in anything which may serve to throw light upon any matter connected with my own family, I shall be prepared to make such terms as may be fair and equitable between us."

He paused again for a reply.

No answer.

"What do you consider your intelligence worth? You are willing, I suppose, to part with it for a consideration?"

"No."

This looked very unpromising for the success of his visit; but he returned to the attack.

"You say you know all about the matter that I am alluding to, and yet you are not willing to part with what you know."

The old man nodded his head in token of acquiescence.

"Not even for a liberal equivalent?"

"No."

He was at a loss how to proceed.

"And may I ask why not?" he said at length.

Again no answer. Irritating old man—very! So much so that his visitor began to lose his temper a little, and to grow sarcastic.

"There are means," he said, "of obliging people to furnish information if they are not willing to do it of their own accord."

The other party did not appear to be the least moved by the prospect of the tortures which might be presumed to await him.

"You have the opportunity of making good use of your knowledge now. I'm ready to pay for it."

The man might have been deaf and dumb from his birth, for all the impression Philip's observation seemed to make upon him.

"You *shall* give it up, old man!" Philip cried at last, his patience now quite exhausted. "I'll make you give it up!" and the fiendish look with which he spoke the words ought to have roused the man from his dogged silence; but it didn't. He only turned round towards the desk, and began busying himself with the papers which were strewed about.

"You'll repent this!" exclaimed Philip, rising from his chair, and shaking his fist in close proximity to the man's head. "You shall tell every syllable you know—every syllable!" and he apostrophised him as he said so in no very complimentary terms. "As sure as my name is Egerton, I'll have it out of you!"

For the first time since the commencement of their conversation—if a monologue can be called conversation—the stolid features seemed to relax into the faintest of grim smiles, which died away as soon as born, and he was still busy with his papers when Philip slammed the street-door behind him.

Poor Philip! this was a sad blow to your little game. Could anything, indeed, have been more aggravating? To know that the solution of your secret was in the hands of that little fiend of a man, and that you couldn't get at it! But although he was baffled for the present, Philip had no intention of letting the matter rest here. Unfortunately his battalion was under orders for Aldershott almost immediately, so that for the present he should be obliged to postpone the further prosecution of whatever fell intentions he may have entertained in regard to his tormentor. But when he returned in the ensuing month—ah! when he returned! What could be the man's reason for withholding what he might have made a profit from if he had liked? Philip could think of no reason to justify such behaviour on the part of a man of that kind. But it is quite possible that the prospect of obtaining elsewhere even better terms than what Philip might propose was some inducement to him to conceal his knowledge for the present, until he had leisure, after the arrangement of the attorney's affairs, to take up the business for himself,—Philip having kindly furnished him with a clue. It is also possible that he may have taken a dislike to Philip on the occasion of their first acquaintance, and thought him not a likely man to be very liberal in his terms —particularly when he seemed so anxious to better his own prospects to such a slight extent at the expense of his brother. And it is very probable now, after Philip's having tried to bully him, that that dogged temper will nourish a hostility towards Mr. Philip Egerton which will make it still more difficult for the latter to extract any additional particulars from his unwilling mouth.

There were other little points, though, which Philip turned over in his mind after he had cooled a little from his recent vexation. Mrs. Greville evidently knew more about the matter than what she could have gathered from the slight hints which he had dropped in the winter. And now that he thought of it, her agitation when he mentioned the subject had certainly not proceeded from his mention of it, but from some additional disturbing cause within her own mind. This also it should be his business to probe on his return. Lady Belvedere and he were not on speaking terms, and therefore he could not expect to make much out of her—nor out of the woman they had mentioned, in Ireland. How annoying it was to be obliged to leave town just at this interesting juncture! But there was no help for it, and further progress, therefore, as far as he was concerned, was necessarily deferred until his return.

CHAPTER VI.

RACING and betting men are not, as a rule, ball-goers. They find no society in ball-rooms and among ladies. Their attention there is annoyingly distracted from the great business of their lives—the one topic which absorbs their interest being not likely to prove a very attractive subject for conversation to the ordinary run of girls. Many think that it is; and being unable to leave their own groove, try to carry everyone else along with them in it. But the generality find it a bore to be obliged to talk on subjects which have no interest for them, and where they are not able to interlard their utterances with graphic illustrations from the stable or the turf. So they stay away, and prefer a noisy dinner with other kindred spirits who have devoted their lives to the outwitting of their friends, or the public, or themselves, or any chance victim who may be thrown across their path. They sit late, drink much, book more bets, make matches for money which they don't possess or can't afford to lose, are never tired of comparing trials, performances, pedigrees, and prospects; and when at last they do adjourn, it is to some more congenial excitement than may be found in a ball-room; and they go to pass the night in gambling away their health in the fetid atmosphere of some noisome hell.

Such was the kind of life which now found charms in Egerton's eyes, although he had not yet absolutely given up society. There was still a counter-attraction in ball-room crowds which drew him nightly from his orgies, when in town, and varied the monotony of his dissipation.

Blanche Villars' love was the sole influence now which kept alive his self-respect, which counteracted the debasing tendencies of his present occupations, and induced his mind to cling yet awhile to the refinement which turf society soon obliterates.

He heard people saying that she was not looking nearly so well this season—so much paler—sometimes almost ill. And he knew the cause very well, and hated himself for the wretchedness which he knew she suffered on his account. He did, therefore, try to break away sometimes from his unprofitable companionship, and enjoyed doubly by contrast the rapture of repose and calm which he experienced in her society.

Had he seen her brother? she asked, one night, as they were sitting down after dancing. Charlie had a message for him, she believed, from Mr. Rowley.

Harry had not seen him, having been out of town for some days, but had heard that he had called the day before.

"You were at Newmarket?" Blanche said, reproachfully.

"Yes, I was. Are you angry? I promised to give up betting, you know, after the Derby."

He explains that having a book upon

that race, he is not able to give it up before. But he does not say that he is now such a gambler at heart that he would find it very difficult to leave off at any time.

"Did you win last week?" Blanche asks, in a tone where interest is subdued by resignation.

Lost a little, Harry said, as if it was quite indifferent to him whether he lost or won. He didn't, however, consider it necessary to explain what "a little" meant.

"Nothing to signify," he said.

Blanche did not immediately reply, but she turned to him a moment or two after, and said—

"Do you know, I saw in some book, the other day, that gambling was an intellectual excitement only fit for the lowest condition of civilisation."

Could it be that she had been reading up works on the subject, to see if there was any hope of Harry's occupation being a useful or profitable one to him?

He laughed, as he answered—"And you thought of me, and thought that I was a savage, or something equally interesting?"

"No, I didn't think you were a savage exactly; but I thought you ought to do something better."

"Ah! but what?"

"Oh! a man can do anything: you are so different from us—you are so much more independent."

"It's all very well, Miss Villars, to say that we can do anything; but without money it seems to me we can do nothing in this interesting world."

"But you have brains. Surely you can make use of them for some better purpose than making bets."

"Indeed," Harry rejoined, "I've often thought about it; and I don't see one single thing that I can do. There isn't a profession—a gentleman's profession—that one can go into without money."

"But papa always says that there are many things for young men to do who have energy and brains."

"So people always say," he replied;

"but when they come to point out what these many things are, they can't name one. I don't see how anyone is to make a profession for himself without being fairly started."

"But a great many men have done so, haven't they? Men who began with nothing in the world, and afterwards came to be great men."

Oh yes, of course! he admitted that such things had been done. "But then those fellows," he said, "were tremendous swells!" and his modesty would not allow him to admit that the circumstances of their case bore ever so slightly upon his own,— even though Blanche did try to prove to him that they were little men once, without any advantages whatever to start with.

The appearance of Galston in a neighbouring doorway disturbed the even flow of Harry's conversation at this point, and Galston's nearer approach brought an expression to his face which might have afforded some amusement to an observant looker-on.

Since the afternoon when they had clashed in Lady Mary's drawing-room, the latter had redoubled his attentions to Blanche, and had treated Harry, when they occasionally met, with an almost contemptuous nod,—which only expressed the very natural astonishment which he felt at the audacity of an untitled and penniless younger son who could have the face to enter into competition with him for the favour of any girl he chose to like. It was too ridiculous, Galston thought, and he determined to punish his impudence by showing him his position. As yet they had not come to close quarters, or it is not unlikely that Egerton would have taken advantage of the slightest opening to make it quite as hot for his lordship as he could conveniently stand.

Now, when he came up and asked Miss Villars for the next dance, tenderness and condescension were so monstrously blended in his tone, that Harry could scarcely refrain from answering for his partner that she was engaged. And, if decency had only permitted it, he would undoubtedly have considered this a most favourable opportunity for putting into execution those charitable designs which, on a previous occasion of like irritation, he had been led to form in respect to his lordship of Galston.

Decency, however, did not permit, and his lordship sauntered away, postponed till some future dance.

"Do you like Galston?" Harry asked, looking into Blanche's face, and awaiting her reply in some suspense.

She didn't exactly dislike him; thought he was ridiculously conceited, but to her he was always very pleasant.

Harry said nothing, but, like that celebrated parrot of taciturn but contemplative habits, he thought a great deal.

In the first place, he thought Blanche ought to have hated Galston; and, in the next, he was quite sure that he did, if it was only because she did not; and in order to create as far as possible a unanimity of sentiment between them upon this point, he proceeded to abuse that poor young man in so bitter a strain that Blanche looked at him in surprise, for his remarks upon even his friends were generally most good-natured.

He had hardly succeeded in persuading her that her admirer was the incarnation of everything objectionable, when her partner for the next dance came up, and Blanche was obliged, reluctantly, to break off their short enjoyment. But she left so regretful a look behind, that he sat on for a little while longer to feast upon the sweets which it contained, and to extract all kinds of imaginary and delightful meaning, which it pleased him much to dwell upon. Rising, at length, with a sigh of resignation, he strolled towards the ball-room door, watched her for awhile from a distance, and then went away to an early bed—having to be up at an unusually early hour the following morning, to get down to a distant race-course in time for the first race.

A couple of days afterwards Villars met him at the door of the club as he was emerging with an open letter in his hand, and a smile on his face.

"Why, Harry, old boy, how are you?" exclaimed Charlie. "I thought we were never going to meet. I've been to your lodgings I don't know how many times to find you."

Harry explained that his engagements now took him from town a good deal; and then, after a little further conversation, handed over the still open letter to his friend.

"That's rather good, isn't it?—an epistle from a friend at Cambridge."

This friend was a politely letter-writing dun, who had addressed him in the following touching strain:—

"Sir,

"As you have not thought me worthy of a reply to the last letters I wrote to you, I must now address you plainly, and deal seriously with you. ('Sounds as if he was telling you to go and wait in the fourth-form room,' Charlie said.) I have several pressing accounts to settle which must be paid; and as I have always to meet my commercial transactions at the expiration of so short a period as three months, you may be sure I cannot afford the credit which you seem to take.

In your only letter you say that you are not in a 'position.' ('What on earth does that mean?') If I have any understanding at all, this is anything but the proper thing. You were wrong to get in debt if you had no means of paying; and I am simply surprised at such conduct."—

"Most upright dun! Who is he?"

"Go on," Harry said; "the terrible consequences have to come yet, and the injured feelings."

"Now, sir" (the letter continued), "I shall commence proceedings on Wednesday, the next ultimo, if you do not pay me by that time. I do not like the manner of your treatment of me, for is it *reasonable* for a tradesman to give such credit? and can he bear such losses?—ask yourself a Question.

"If your account is not settled by next Wednesday, do not blame me. I am innocent. I have done my duty as a tradesman, and I must now leave the matter with you and my solicitor.

"I am, sir, &c., &c."

"Neatly put, isn't it?" said Harry, when Villars had finished reading.

"Very; I like the idea of his doing his duty as a man and a tradesman. Are you going to pay him?"

"Can't, my dear boy, at present," answered Egerton, quietly tearing up the letter, and scattering the fragments in the gutter. "I generally wait till the first lawyer's letter arrives, and then answer them. They don't get much change out of me by sending letters to the club, and only one or two of them know my father's address, which doesn't do them much good either. I'm sorry for some of them who are really hard up; but I can't help it, you know. I'd pay them all like a shot if I could."

"By the way," he continued presently, after refusing to take advantage of Villars' offer to lend him money if he wanted any, "your sister told me the other night that you had some message for me; from Rowley, I think."

"Yes, I was going to tell you," rejoined Villars; and he proceeded to extract from his pocket-book the address which Rowley had given to him of Harry's namesake, accompanying it with what details he knew respecting him.

Egerton was all attention. Independently of the first impulse of benevolence which would have prompted him to hunt up the man at once, and see what could be done for him, he had the additional motive of curiosity to know what connection he might be of his own; and, further, and more important still, the possibility of his being able to throw some light upon his own uncertain position. Accordingly, after hearing all that Villars had to say upon the subject, he announced his intention of proceeding eastwards at once; said he was interested, in answer to Charlie's slight look of surprise at his promptitude, promised to meet him at Prince's in the afternoon, if he got back safe, called a Hansom, jumped into it, and was soon rattling along Coventry Street, *en route* for the slums of the East End.

He had not much to relate when they met again in the afternoon. The old woman who kept the house said that he had left there a couple of months and more,—which it was a good riddance, it was. *She* didn't want no lodgers as couldn't pay their rent. It was hard upon a widder woman to be kep' out of her own, &c., &c. On the sight of half-a-crown, however, she had come round;—didn't know but what she might be able to find him, if it was made worth her while; had said that he was a civil-spoken man enough, although he was a bit high and mighty for one as hadn't a shilling to call his own, and eventually had agreed to find him. Harry was to return in the course of a few days to hear what result her labours had produced (she probably knowing where he was to be found all the time), and, of course, to pay her. It was no pleasant prospect having to do all that dirt and smell over again; but the end was a worthy one, he thought, even putting aside altogether the possibility of benefit to himself arising therefrom, and so it should be done. And until he found leisure and opportunity for doing it, an undefined presentiment that this man would have some future hand in bringing to a crisis the mystery which he had lately hung around himself, would keep forcing itself in upon his thoughts even in the midst of the most exciting scenes, and kept him in a nervous state of anticipation,—for no reason at all, except that he had heard of a man of his own name being in a strange position, and he didn't know who he was.

CHAPTER VII.

Of course he was sitting next to Miss Grant. For what other reason had Lady Belvedere asked him to dinner except that he might sit next to Miss Grant? And next to Miss Grant, therefore, having taken her down to dinner, you see that he is now sitting. She, at all events, was not displeased with the arrangement, and, on the whole, I don't think Harry was either; for Cornelia was as pleasant a dinner neighbour as you often get saddled with in that lottery of dinner-pairs.

Besides being able to talk, she had other qualifications for being a good neighbour. She enjoyed her dinner as much as she did your conversation; and, therefore, you were allowed to eat your soup when other people were doing the same, instead of being entertained during that time with a flow of nonsense which scarified the roof of your mouth, or sent away your plate almost untouched. She showed a similar forbearance and judgment throughout the whole of the meal, and the result was manifest in the evenness with which conversation flowed in the intervals.

With Egerton she had wandered over several indifferent topics already, and had now fallen back upon their visit to Belvedere. Was fond of country-house visiting,—got to know people so much better in that way,—never became intimate with any one in London.

"No; and it's difficult enough to keep up one's intimacies," Harry said. "I declare I hardly ever see my best friends in London. They're always rushing about so from one thing to another that they haven't time to stop and speak to you. I suppose it's the same with ladies?"

More so, Cornelia thought. Young ladies were so busied about their dress, and their partners, and their balls,—in fact, their friendships were only a common interest in these things.

"I suppose there are real friendships sometimes amongst girls?" Harry said. "One always hears them talking with most extravagant affection about each other."

"Never lasting ones," said Miss Grant. "Women were made for love, not friendship. Those very great friendships between girls always end in smoke, or a quarrel, or something equally conclusive,—the marriage, perhaps, of one of them."

"I was rather surprised," Harry resumed, after a pause, "to hear a girl say the other day that she had a number of very great friends, but that she never wrote to one of them, and yet she was just as glad to see them again when they met. Do you believe in friendship being kept up without corresponding?"

"In some cases I dare say it may be. That's what I call real constancy—meeting again with the same feelings after a long silence and separation. Girls, however, very seldom allow their feelings to go through that ordeal. They generally write sheets of nonsense to each other every week, and have two or three intimate correspondents going on at the same time, signing themselves by every endearing term to be found in the dictionary of superlatives."

Harry didn't think it was possible to have more than one real friend at a time; and Miss Grant agreed with him. "But girls' friends," she said, "are not real friends. A girl calls another a dear friend who praises her dress, tells her all the pretty things people say of her, and flatters her vanity. That is a very different kind of friendship from what I conceive men's to be."

"But you must have friends yourself; do they say pretty things to you?"

Cornelia was happy to say that all girls were not made up of silliness and vanity. Cornelia, you see, was a very superior person.

"But I never had any great friends," she continued. "I always distrusted the continuance of their friendship, and so I never allowed my feelings to run away with me."

"Strong-minded person indeed!" Harry thought. But he did not think that it was probably to the considerable amount of thought which, from the nature of her position, Miss Grant had been in the habit of bestowing upon herself, that her scepticism in regard of friendship might be traced. Cornelia, though in many ways a very estimable person, had grown up in the belief that there was but one Cornelia in the world; and that that singular person, from being the absolute owner of landed property in her own right, was a person to be very much considered, both by herself, and by everybody around her. And, therefore, after paying the rather exaggerated consideration which she thought due to herself, she had not enough material over to make such an exchange as would cement a real *bonâ fide* friendship. Arguing, accordingly, from her own deficiency in the self-forgetfulness which is the chief ingredient in friendship as in love, she entertained those views on the durability of friendship which she has expressed above, and which have evoked a certain peculiar admiration from her neighbour.

"You advocate giving votes to women, don't you?" he said, abruptly enough, after a short pause.

"Certainly I do. But why do you ask?"

Not having heard his opinion upon her last remark, Miss Grant was perhaps justified in thinking that the subject had been changed rather suddenly.

"Only because you said just now," Harry rejoined, "that most girls were made up of silliness and vanity. Do you think the woman who only lives from one season to another, or from one ball to another, and hasn't an idea beyond her dress, would be a very safe depositary for the privileges of the suffrage, as they say?"

"Girls would not come under the head of women. And for that matter, there are many girls who live for something more than mere pleasure-hunting and frivolous amusement."

"Oh! I know," Harry broke in, "a great many always say they hate London, and long to be in the country. But do you suppose they mean it?"

"Some do. Some girls' tastes are simple enough. But their preferring the country to the town is no proof of their superiority. They may, of course, do a great deal of good there. But if everyone were to bury themselves in the country, it would be a great misfortune for society generally. Marriage is the chief end of a woman's life— and a man's too, as far as that goes—and the assembling of people in London very much conduces to that end. There is no reason, because they come to London, that they should devote themselves exclusively to pleasure while they are there."

Harry looked curiously at her as she enunciated her sentiments upon woman's aim in life, but a philosophic repose was all that her face expressed; and he went on to draw her yet further on the subject of woman's rights and mission. He knew he was getting a little out of his depth on these subjects, and therefore merely suggested ideas to be corrected.

"But if the world was made for man," he said, "and woman only created as an extra, to keep him company, and be subject to him, don't you think the government of the world ought to be left to men?"

History, Miss Grant said, told of women as renowned as any men, who had governed great nations with signal success. Woman's intellect had not been given to her for nothing. And if she was capable of forming opinions on questions of government and politics, she had as much right to have her voice heard as any other member of the community interested in its own good government.

All this was not an answer to Harry's modest question. But then, if Miss Grant had given a direct answer, and had not avoided doing so by arguing beside the question, she would have been no woman.

Egerton, however, demurred to the capability of women for forming opinions on questions of State. Women, he said, in his humble opinion, could only see one side of a question generally, and they were much more easily carried away by prejudice, and influenced by trifling considerations, which a man's stronger reason would reject. Their intellects, too, were of a lower order, more superficial, not capable of taking in a broad view of any subject. (He was getting on as a philosopher.)

"I beg your pardon," returned Cornelia, decidedly, thinking that she had him there. "It is always acknowledged that a woman's natural intelligence is much quicker than a man's."

"Yes, perhaps so," Harry admitted. "But what I mean is, that your intellects are not solid enough for the heavy work that men's minds are engaged upon. A woman, now, never can stick to the point in arguing. Very few women, I should think, could sustain a closely-reasoned argument. And there are a great many things, I fancy, in science and philosophy, for instance, that they couldn't understand at all."

"And why, Mr. Egerton?—will you tell

me? One of the profoundest writers of the day is a woman. You find women translating the Greek classics—women engaged in all kinds of intellectual work—and women, you may depend upon it, very often originating the measures for which their husbands get the credit."

Harry smiled. About that he could offer no opinion; but as to intellectual work, women who shone in that department were very rare, he thought; and he was very glad of it. "You know, Miss Grant," he said, "I always think that a woman ought not to know too much—science and all that sort of thing."

"Why should you think so?"

"Well, I don't know exactly. Don't you think they're more men's pursuits?"

"But if a woman's intellect is able to understand them, I can't conceive why she may not know them as well as a man."

Egerton could give no reason against it. But, though unable to explain himself as clearly as he would have liked, the general impression still remained upon his mind, that high intellectual cultivation was never meant for women. His idea of woman was connected with all the softer, gentler duties of life, and a highly intellectual female appeared to his hazy comprehension a kind of *lusus naturæ*.

Great mental culture and studious habits are not necessarily incompatible with the performance of a woman's natural obligations as wife or mother or sister. But women of intellect are seldom very domestic women, and while they are striving after a knowledge which only in exceptional cases can be productive of benefit to any but themselves, they are missing the opportunity of playing well the part for which they are especially fitted, and for which they were specially intended. The society of a really clever woman (except that she generally talks too much) is most attractive when you know that her mind has not been cultivated at the expense of her sympathies and affections. When it has been so, her attractiveness is counteracted by the consciousness that there is something anomalous in her which offends while it pleases—gives more offence, perhaps, than pleasure, as everything which is untrue to nature always does. You look upon her as a kind of prodigy, and feel the same kind of interest in watching her movements, and listening to her talk, as you do in looking at the fat woman of the show, or the woman with a tail, or any other curious freak of nature.

Harry Egerton, however, had never analysed his ideas upon this subject, and only knew that a very clever woman always made him feel rather small. And having a proper sense of his dignity as a man, the suggestion of inferiority jarred upon his nerves. It never struck him that the acquisition of knowledge for himself might have the effect of placing him in the position of superiority which he claimed. The levelling-up principle had never come home to him.

Miss Grant had been pleased to find that he had some ideas on general subjects, and she told Lady Belvedere in the drawing-room afterwards that she thought him very intelligent for a young man of the kind; that he had a good deal more sense than most of the uninteresting youths with whom it had been her fate to converse from time to time. Of course Lady Belvedere passed this on to her nephew, and of course Harry was proud and delighted to hear that a person of Miss Grant's strong common sense had pronounced him to be not absolutely a fool.

Lady Belvedere was going on to a ball at Lady Emily L'Estrange's, and as Harry was also going in that direction, she had given him a seat in her carriage.

"When are you going to propose to Cornelia Grant?" she had said, abruptly.

Harry laughed, and said that he really had not thought of it,—didn't think he could undertake so much mind.

And Lady Belvedere had said that she was very clever and sensible, and would make an excellent wife, and that Harry must not forget the money, and the place in the country, and all that. And then she had repeated, with embellishments of her own,

Miss Grant's remarks upon his intelligence, and told him that there was no doubt but what she liked him, for she had said so more than once.

"But perhaps," her ladyship continued, "she has not seen enough of you yet. Best not to be in too great a hurry."

Harry made some joking answer, and then his aunt inquired how he came to be going to Lady Emily's—they didn't seem to be very great friends at Belvedere.

"She must ask some younger sons," Harry said. "But she never thinks me worth speaking to when we meet. What a vulgar woman she is!"

"She ought not to be," Lady Belvedere answered; "a duke's daughter."

"She doesn't get her manners from him, though. He's the most courteous old bird I know," Harry rejoined.

"They say she is trying hard to get Lord Galston for that eldest girl of hers," said Lady Belvedere.

"I don't think she will," replied her nephew, shortly.

Lady Belvedere thought the second by far the nicest, and Harry very much agreed with her; Florence L'Estrange was a great friend of his; the other snubbed him,—perhaps because he never asked her to dance; more probably, because he had neither money nor title to recommend him. Up to the present time Miss L'Estrange had laid herself out for an establishment to no purpose; all her little arts had been practised in vain, and disappointment made her now more than ever snappish to younger sons, and more than ever complaisant to elder ones.

It is a beautiful sight, a scheming girl! An ambitious mother is bad enough in all conscience!—but to see a girl putting off all the charms of freshness, and innocence, and modest reserve, and quiet self-respect, which one is wont to associate with early womanhood, and to see her deliberately scheming, calculating, plotting, to attract the gauds of position or wealth; cultivating the meanness, and untruthfulness, and suspicious, intriguing, hypocritical littleness of the woman of the world — oh! it's a very charming sight! and it is one that may be seen every day in London drawing-rooms, where English ladies go to school to learn all the most noble, and elevated, and useful qualities of their sex.

But Lady Belvedere's carriage has drawn up before Lady Emily's door in Eaton Square, and she is being assisted to alight by an officious and impertinent linkman, who professes to be glad to see her ladyship looking so well.

A couple of fingers from Lady Emily, and Harry is in the middle of a crowd again, looking anxiously round for the one face which he came to see.

Florence L'Estrange happens to be standing near him, sees his eager glance, and tells him wickedly that she has not come yet. A playful conversation ensues; she goes away to dance, and Harry retires to the top of the stairs to wait,—looking on, meanwhile, with a mixture of amusement and disgust at a passage of arms then going on between the eldest Miss L'Estrange and that modest, shy, retiring young man, Lord Galston,—who, for some reason best known to himself, has turned up at this ball much earlier than is customary with such eligible young men. He usually likes to think that the ladies are all waiting for him, and strolls in, later on in the evening, with other similarly eligible spirits.

On the present occasion he had been inveigled by Lady Emily into a duty dance with the eldest daughter of the house, and very pleasant he appeared to find it.

The girl is trying to blush. Harry can see that she is saying, "Oh! Lord Galston!" with a deprecatory sniff at her bouquet. And from the indifferent air which Galston assumes, he conjectures that the last shaft has been followed up by a compliment. A languishing, semi-tender look replies to one of those very ordinary platitudes in which Lord Galston's *métier* lies; and then a water-party is gradually unfolded to his delighted gaze. Mamma would be so glad to see him. They were to dine at Maidenhead; yes, next Sunday. He really *must* come. Indeed,

Miss L'Estrange would not go if Lord Galston was not there. The fan was here slightly raised to hide a watchful face, and the dance coming to an end, Miss L'Estrange told her mamma, as she passed the door, that Lord Galston had promised to come,—wasn't it too charming of him?

Lady Emily thought it was quite too charming, and joined her praises to those of her daughter in an harmonious duet of flattery, which floated in indifferently upon the victim's already surfeited ear, gently helping to keep alive that flame of self-conceit within, which would have burned quite as brightly with half the attention which it now received.

Galston stayed late at Lady Emily L'Estrange's ball—it was a good ball, he said. But if you had asked Egerton, he would have told you that it was the dullest ball he had ever been at; would have abused Lady Emily, and her house, and her company, and everything belonging to that ball. And all because Galston had been beforehand with him in engaging Blanche Villars to dance, and had looked at him triumphantly as he passed. Galston didn't mean to show that there was any cause for triumph, but his face couldn't help expressing it as he passed with Blanche on his arm. And then Harry had watched them talking, and had seen Blanche laughing and looking interested in what Galston had been saying, and after that he didn't ask her to dance with him, but sneaked about the stairs and the supper-room, and avoided her, and finally saw Galston take her to her carriage, and come back looking so pleased with himself that he could have knocked him down on the spot.

Miss L'Estrange, too, had noticed Galston's attentions to Miss Villars; and Miss L'Estrange had given it as her opinion that Florence's friend, that Blanche Villars, was an artful creature; that it grieved her to see such depravity in one so young and so fair —no, she didn't say fair; but that she needn't hope, with all her artifice, to catch Lord Galston; Miss L'Estrange, indeed, flattering herself that *her* snares had been laid with a most promising prospect of success.

Harry might have been sorry, perhaps, for having avoided Blanche this evening, if he had known, as he walked moodily down the square in the early morning, that she was even then worrying her mind to account for the coldness which he had shown to her, and thinking of him as fondly as ever notwithstanding.

But how was he to know it? All he knew was that he had seen her dancing with Galston before she had done so with him, and actually not looking bored; on the contrary, smiling. He had taken her to her carriage, too. It was enough; his affections were blighted; his love was being trampled upon; and he strode on savagely past St. Peter's Church, past Buckingham Palace, down the Mall, in the direction of his rooms.

The sky in the east was clear with the coming dawn. The early birds were chirping in the trees; and the morning air was cool and fresh as he walked, hat in hand, through the silence, down the rows of trees, and past the sleeping forms upon the benches. But neither fresh morning air, nor bright clear sky, nor chirp of birds, nor even sleeping forms on benches, or peeler on the prowl, had interest or charm for Harry now. Misery's cold apathy had settled on his mind; and he stalks on to his rooms a walking monument of woe.

Pity the sorrows of a poor young man. Remove his razors; see him into bed; draw the curtains, and tuck him up with his pretty jealousy.

CHAPTER VIII.

Is there no balm in Gilead, no relief for a broken heart, to be found in the affections and the money of an heiress?

Surely Cornelia's rent-roll would have bound up the lacerated organ, and her love made amends for the loss of that cruel Blanche, if it was true that she had really gone.

I'm sure that Cornelia, if she had been asked, was prepared with all the solace which the case required; for even strong-minded people, who don't allow their feelings to run away with them, occasionally find that their reins have not been strong enough, and that they are hurrying at full gallop, in spite of themselves, to the edge of that dreaded precipice.

So it was with Cornelia Grant.

Not easy of access to men of any age, her particular aversion hitherto had been younger sons, who are supposed to be more inclined to matrimony than their more experienced fellows. But Harry Egerton's indifference had piqued her vanity at first, and then his frankness and unaffected manner had engaged her interest, his good looks won her liking, and his sensible sentiments on things in general given her a good excuse for feeling a pleasure in his company, until she had actually almost allowed herself to be hurried away to the verge of the steep declivity before mentioned. Of course she would never have acknowledged to herself that she, Cornelia Grant—a person who looked upon men in general as interested, false, and deceitful—that she was actually in love with one of these objectionable creatures. But, nevertheless, whenever she met Egerton in any public place or private entertainment, her eyes would wander off in his direction, and her expression would seem to denote that she was mentally appraising all the various good qualities and attractive parts which went to make up that interesting entity, Henry Egerton. So that if Henry Egerton could only persuade himself that he was really a blighted being, and were to turn for comfort to the arms of his Cornelia, there is every probability that those arms would not reject him, and that he might be the happy possessor of that eligible property for life.

But at present Henry Egerton has failed to persuade himself that his future existence is to be a blank—he proposes to give it another trial; and, therefore, he is not yet in a fit state of preparation for putting his head into a money-bag. What he may do at some future time, under the overpowering influence of inauspicious circumstances, remains to be determined. And from the heavy pressure upon his barometer at present, one might not unnaturally infer that storms may be expected soon which will compel him to run into any port which promises a refuge; for, from a speculative point of view, he had been a complete failure ever since that unlucky visit to Punchestown. Even pigeon-shooting, which he thought must win him back some of his lost money, had gone against him. A judicious friend had said, "Don't go down till three o'clock, when you can see pretty well how they're shooting. Choose a hot day, when the birds are lazy, and stupid with being shut up so long in the baskets. Then pick your guns, and lay your two to one like a man!" It sounded a good recipe enough for winning; but he had not followed it out in every particular. Insinuating book-makers behind had led him on to back the gun every time. Whenever he was there the shooting was unusually bad; and he had invariably come away a poorer man (on paper) than he had gone there. But then he never paid. So what did it matter, after all? He still had his champagne and other necessaries when he entertained himself at dinner, and lived in every way as a gentleman of his independent fortune might be expected to live.

Wedged in a doorway one evening, unable to move for the crush of surrounding bodies, he heard some remarks upon the kind of life which men in his position were in the habit of leading; which remarks, absurd though they were, he could not help applying rather uncomfortably to himself.

Lord Staunton was the speaker; and he appeared to hold most curiously heterodox and old-fashioned opinions on this, as on many other points. He was on this particular evening performing the unnatural function of chaperon to his daughter, in her ladyship's place; and the daughter was at the moment dancing with a younger son, who was generally supposed to have been "broke" several times already—Skindles, in fact, that merry, reckless, devil-may-care young profligate.

He it was who provoked Lord Staunton to launch into the absurdities about to be recorded. For it puzzled him, Lord Staunton said, to know how young fellows like that managed to get along at all. He had been credibly informed that that youngster had not a sixpence to his name, and yet he saw him driving his tea-cart, and dining expensively at his club, living in every way as if he was the eldest son to an extensive property. "Who pays for it all? that's what I want to know. They can't live like princes for nothing."

"It never is paid for," replied his younger neighbour, "unless their fathers are mulcted. It only lasts for a year or two, and then they disappear."

"Well, I call it nothing less than downright robbery," rejoined Lord Staunton; "a regular system of imposition and fraud. When I was a young man we had some notions of honour, but the young men of the present day don't seem to understand anything of the kind. Society must be in a pretty state to tolerate and countenance such fellows."

"Oh!" said the other, "a man only begins to 'live' nowadays when the hammer is over his house." And he adduced one or two notorious examples in proof of the assertion.

The names mentioned only added a stimulus to Lord Staunton's indignation. "It's a scandalous thing," he said with emphasis, " to see fine properties brought into the market in this way, and old names dragged in the dirt by these miserable fellows, who have no idea of what is due to their position. And it is not only their own worthless selves that they are disgracing, but their shame stigmatises all the rest of their class—brings discredit upon all of us. And, depend upon it, the profligate conduct of these poor fools of spendthrifts will be a most powerful lever for Radicals and levellers to work against the upper classes. It will all tend to help us on towards democracy, and God knows we are going in that direction fast enough already. People don't know their position now as they used to thirty or forty years ago. Then there was a line of demarcation between the gentleman and the blackguard. That seems to have disappeared now. And other distinctions will very soon follow."

His neighbour being a member of the House of Commons who votes on the Liberal side (Conservative side I suppose one ought to say now) on the subject of

Reform, prefers not to argue the question from that particular point of view; asks whether there has not always been extravagance in former periods as well as at the present—Crockford's for instance?

"Never to the same extent," Lord Staunton replied. "At Crockford's the rules of the place forbade it. And though men gambled high, it was never in sums approaching to the stakes which we are told are common on the turf nowadays."

"I wonder if the richer men ever think of the responsibility they incur by leading young fellows to bet so far above their means," said the other presently. "I know several who began by just dabbling in it, and were gradually led on to increase their stakes, and now, without any capital whatever to fall back upon, bet in their thousands as coolly as Crœsus himself might. If they win, they live jovially till they lose; and when they lose, they don't pay."

"Monstrous!" ejaculated Lord Staunton, who further considered that this betting mania was one of the greatest evils of the day (what a strange man it was!), and that if anything called for legislation, this was a subject which required immediate consideration more than any other which could be named.

A member, fresh from the House, being borne up against them here, interrupted the conversation with news of the night's proceedings, while Harry was carried away with the stream of retiring dancers, digesting the pill which he had been obliged to swallow.

One ought, perhaps, to admit that, since the very recent period at which the events narrated in these pages occurred, there has been a decided improvement upon the turf in this one respect. Betting is not now carried on by youngsters to the ridiculous extent which was in vogue a year or two ago. Prudence has appeared again, and taught them the folly of their ways. But let no one suppose that, with prudence, a sense of honour has returned. Such a thing is only known as an abstract term to the men of this generation. The instinct of the gentleman has disappeared. A man who cheats at a pigeon match now, instead of being cut by every gentleman of his acquaintance, finds apologists, not only amongst his friends, but even in the press. And the apology is significant enough. It was hard lines that he should be detected, and found fault with by some punctilious persons, when everybody else (so they said) was in the habit of behaving in the same open and honourable manner. We are coming to the state of things which Thucydides described in Greece at the time of the Peloponnesian war, when the very names of things were changed, new meanings attached to old words, the code of dishonour made the code of honour, and the knave held in high repute for his cleverness, while the honourable man was an object of suspicion. On the turf one expects to hear of every mean artifice and low rascality being practised with impunity; for there, of course, we know that blackguardism and cheating form the chief excitement of the greater number of its supporters. They are the recognised principles of the sport. But it is rather startling to one's prejudices to be told that a man can deliberately cheat in any other department of sport, and not suffer in the esteem of his friends,—to hear, on the contrary, that he is considered an ill-used man because everyone will not see his eccentricity in the light in which, according to the habits of the time, it ought to be viewed. Any modern Juvenal, looking upon society at the present day, would have good cause for saying "*difficile est satiram non scribere.*"

Lord Staunton would no doubt have attributed the decay of honour to the same cause which, in his opinion, had brought about a deterioration in the manners of the day. He would have said that it was all the product of that pestilent money-worship, which was bringing into society large numbers of men who had been brought up in circumstances where traditional honour was unknown, and who were gradually infecting the higher classes with all the ill qualities which characterise the low-born money-maker. I would not have you sure that he was altogether wrong.

Evil communications undoubtedly do corrupt good manners; if you want a proof of it, just consider the difference which has taken place in Egerton's character during the last few months. See how little he thinks of honour now, how careless he is of the interests of his friends, how the selfishness of the money-hunter is growing upon him, what small scruple he feels now in taking advantage of any questionable opening for the furtherance of his mercenary schemes, and how coarse excitement and degrading associations are overpowering former refinement of feeling and crushing out that too delicate sensitiveness which might stand in the way of his interest.

However, deteriorated though he was, there was still a good deal left to like in him, and amid all his necessities, he had not forgotten the troubles of his namesake.

Another visit had been paid to his former lodging. And its owner, having made sure of her reward, had despatched a ragged urchin to conduct Harry to the spot where

Captain Egerton, as she called him, was now to be found.

After threading an intricate labyrinth of loathsome alleys, and by-streets, where sights that filled him with shuddering horror met his eye at every turn (and where, by the way, he was conscious of an unpleasant feeling of insecurity), he followed his conductor into a filthy court, where he had to pick his way through uncleanness of every repulsive kind, and through grimy urchins yelling in ragged dirt, who jeered him as he passed—and arrived at last at the foot of a dark and rickety stair.

His cicerone, in choice terms, summoned the proprietor; and an old crone appeared at the top of the stairs, and demanded their business.

This having been explained in the respectful terms which were natural to the locality, some good round oaths were showered down in return, and the gentleman was desired to walk up.

The boy having been retained by the promise of prospective remuneration, and Cerberus having been propitiated with a sop, Harry desired to know if any person of the name of Egerton lived there. In reply, the door of a deserted lodging-room was thrown open, and the old hag, pointing to an emaciated wretch, who was the sole occupant of the room, asked, gruffly, if that was him, and, leaving Harry to find out for himself, shambled away to her gin-bottle again.

The miserable creature, who appeared to be in the last stage of physical weakness, looked up feebly as Harry approached, and replied, in a scarcely audible voice, that Egerton was his name.

Harry explained how it was that he had found him, hoped that he was not too late to be of some service to him, and asked how he came by his name, what his Christian name was, and how he had come into his present position?

A faint flicker of reviving hope lighted up the sunken eyes, as he expressed, in broken sentences, his thanks, and said that his name was Frank, and that he had formerly been in the army.

"Frank!" Harry repeated; "in the army! Where did you live? Who was your father?"

This point was explained too; and Harry seemed lost in astonishment.

"You never can be the Frank I remember when I was quite a boy! He——"

"The very same, sir," broke in the other, in a voice stronger than before.

"But he's dead! I've heard my father say so often. He went abroad, and died out there somewhere."

"He did go abroad," the other said, "but he didn't die, sir. It would have been well for him, indeed, if he had. He's speaking to you now."

Harry explained who he was himself, and how he was, as the other knew, his not very distant cousin; and then inquired how it was that he had allowed himself to be reduced in this way without applying to any of his relations for relief.

The old story which Rowley had heard was repeated; but Harry's father was excepted from the rest of the relations who had shut their doors against him. He had been away from England at the time, or else Frank Egerton knew that he would have been differently treated by him. He had been wild and extravagant himself, and therefore he would have made allowances for another. But he had never gone near any of them after that time; he wouldn't run the risk of being turned away again.

"But what have you been doing, then, all this time?" Harry asked. "Did you get work?"

An odd job of copying he used to get at first, or something of that kind, which kept him in some sort of comfort. "But it wasn't easy to get work without a reference," he said; "and it was harder for one who had been a gentleman, for they don't like to take a man who might pretend to be better than his employer."

Then he had worked in the docks, until he lost his thumb by the falling of a beam. And then work fell off there. "And sometimes," he said, "I worked as a porter, and often I got no work at all; and then I was sorely pinched, sir, and had to sleep where I could, and beg a bit of bread in the streets."

Harry wondered that he had survived it all these years, and looked at him with a kind of incredulous astonishment.

"Thank God," he said, "I was able to keep from drinking! and it's hard to do in the middle of dirt like this. It's the easiest way to forget your misery. Only that when I could," he continued, "I kept to the ground-floor, I don't think I'd be talking to you now, Mr. Henry."

There was something rather touching in the humility which now added a Mr. to the boy he had played with on equal terms in days long past.

"Why?" Harry asked, seeing that he paused with a meaning, sad expression.

"When you're close to the street," he said, as if he wished to avoid the subject, "you can go out if you are tired. But when you're up that height above the ground, and nearly mad with hunger—God help you then!"

Harry knew what he meant now, and was

rather awed at being brought directly face to face with despair such as he had never attempted to realise before. He was sure, he said, that his father would do something for him, if he only knew how he was circumstanced. "But, unfortunately," he added, "I'm not on good terms with my father now, so I'm not sure exactly how to let him know."

"Never quarrel with your father, sir!" exclaimed the other with a feeble energy, "if it's not presuming in me to give you advice. It was that which brought me to what I am, and I deserve it—after all these long years of trouble I can still say that I deserve it."

"I'm sure I have no wish to," Harry replied. "But I'll see what can be done, and send you a line—where?—to the nearest post-office; unless you like to go to my father yourself. You know his house in Eaton Place?"

He did, well. But he thought he wouldn't go. If Harry was kind enough to interest himself in his behalf he was extremely grateful. But it was better perhaps, after all, to let him drag out the remainder of his life where he was. It would not be for long.

Harry, however, thought otherwise, and having arranged an address where he should write to him, he left a sovereign in his eager hand, and had gained the door again before he was aware that there was another inmate to the room. This, then, accounted for the sovereign having been hidden away so quickly! And he paused a moment, in doubt what he should do about securing to his cousin the possession of his wealth. As no remedy immediately presented itself, he passed on, did not break his neck down the stairs, regained the court, and found the boy waiting to conduct him back again to his Hansom.

When the creak of his footstep had died away, that other form in the corner uncoiled and shuffled quickly across to where Frank Egerton was attempting to rise to go in search of food. Under any circumstances the wild expression of that woman's face would have been an unpleasant subject for contemplation. But now, with money in his possession, and too weak to defend it, Frank Egerton's newly raised soul sank within him.

Robbery, however, was not apparently her present object; for she seized him by the arm, and asked excitedly whether she had heard his name aright? Had he said his name was Egerton—Egerton?

On receiving an answer in the affirmative, she pointed eagerly in the direction of the door, "And he!—he!—is his name Egerton? and did he say his father's name was Philip? and his brother's name was Philip? and his own name!—what did he say his own name was?—quick, man, quick! tell me!"

The hurried and excited tones in which her questions were uttered were made more bewildering by a strong Scotch accent. And as the other hastened to satisfy her upon every point, he felt an unpleasant misgiving that he was at that moment in the clutch of a mad woman. But when, after obtaining Mr. Egerton's address, she burst into a wild shout of laughter, and declared that she should be a lady yet, and then proceeded to give such good general reasons for such a wild assertion, he was obliged to confess that there was some method at all events in her madness.

This was the same woman who had passed off her dying husband upon Harry in the park some months before. She had recognised him as he passed through the court; followed him up the stairs, and listened to his interview with his cousin, while waiting to pour some other tale of woe into his benevolent ear. No fabricated tale, however, was needed now, after hearing what she had heard; and it was only the calculating prudence of her race which restrained her from arresting him as he passed, and communicating what, after having made sure of her facts, she will no doubt ere long disclose.

CHAPTER IX.

WHILE the Fates are at work upon Harry's destiny, he is returning to the West again, musing over the strange chance which should have led him to unearth a relation in such a place; pondering over the career which had been unfolded for his warning; wondering whether he should ever be telling a similar story; and, while rejoicing in the prospect of being able to relieve the man's distress, lamenting that the link in his own history, which he had hoped for from that visit, had not been supplied. All was hazy and unsatisfactory as before—certainty of any sort would have been better than the state of undefined doubt and apprehension which hung over him at present. What with this, and the nervous anticipation caused by the near approach of the Derby, and the gnawing of a jealousy which increased rather than diminished in intensity the more unfounded his reason proved it to be—with all these equally exacting emotions always struggling for recognition in his mind, he had so much to occupy his thoughts when he was alone, that he never was alone if he could help it now. Constant variety and constant turbulent excitement were his only repose.

The soothing influence of Rossini's music had been sought one evening to lull disturbing thoughts into a temporary calm.

The curtain has fallen upon the second act of *Il Barbiere;* the applause has died away, and the echoes are whispering to themselves about the dome. The stalls wake up into life; dresses are rustling; men are standing up to show their well-brushed hair, and putting themselves into posture against the chairs behind, or looking pretty in the doorways; while ladies have altered their positions, or so prepared themselves in the front of their boxes as may best suit the focus of levelled opera-glasses from below.

Citizens of elaborate coiffure, who have talked through the whole of the preceding act, are talking still, with glasses steadily fixed upon some royal party (the very minutiæ of whose dress they are laying up in their memories for future discussion), or else they are engaged in the most intensely interesting speculation as to who it may be sitting beside some earl or marquis whom they know by sight. There is a stir and bustle and hum of mingled voices and laughter through the house; but Egerton still sits wrapped in the dreamy delight which the last notes of the music have produced, until the mention of a well-known name sent a thrill of interest through his frame, which roused him into active thought again in a moment.

"Doesn't Miss Villars look well to-night?" says a man behind to his friend; and the other directs his glasses to the box where she and her mother are sitting.

"Lovely!" he replies. "I never saw her looking better, I think. She'll be thrown away on that fellow, Galston. Look at him now. Did you ever see such a conceited-looking ass?"

"I suppose it's true she's going to marry him?"

"So they say."

"'Pon my soul!" said the first speaker, who had kept his glasses fixed upon Blanche all the time he was speaking, "I think I could almost make a fool of myself for that girl. I don't know where you'll find another such charming expression as that. I shouldn't mind being in Galston's place this minute."

Galston at that moment was bending down over her, making small conversation, which Blanche was trying very hard to pretend an interest in,—but her thoughts were far away in a stall where she had detected a well-known head, and she was wondering, expecting, hoping that he would come and speak to them.

Harry had listened with a painful interest to the conversation behind him. His face had flushed up with suppressed emotions as he heard the probability of her marriage discussed; and he had bitten his lip to an extent which, under circumstances of a less distracting nature, would have caused him very considerable pain. But what thought had he for physical pain at present? He had turned slowly round, to prolong the agony of uncertainty, or to put off the pain of certainty, and had cast his eyes, with all outward appearance of indifference, towards Lady Mary's box,—and had satisfied himself. There was Blanche, and there was Galston! What further proof was required? Of course he had no right to expect her to refuse such a match as Galston. He had never even told her that he cared for her— never *told* her; no! And then his eye fell upon Lady Belvedere, who was seated not far off, bedecked with diamonds for a smart ball which was to take place that evening. Miss Grant was her only companion. And Harry starts up, and makes for the lobby, passes Lady Mary Villars' name, with lips compressed and a curious sensation in his throat, shakes off acquaintances who wish to detain him, knocks, and enters Lady Belvedere's box.

Lady Belvedere asks what makes him look so ill; and Cornelia, too, professes quite an interest in his health.

Nothing was the matter, Harry said, that he knew of; and he began to make ghastly attempts at lively conversation, and talked so incoherently, that they began to think he had but recently dined. The sidelong glances which, in spite of him, he occasionally cast at an opposite box, were lost upon, or had no meaning for, the two ladies. And when he went away, Lady Belvedere made light of the oddness of his behaviour, afraid that it might have the effect of bringing him down a peg in Cornelia's estimation.

Again he passed the Villars' door, which Galston had just shut behind him; and a sudden impulse made him hesitate for a moment as he passed. He overcame it, and returned to his stall.

Blanche had seen him with Lady Belvedere, and her eyes, to Galston's discontent, would keep wandering in that direction while she feigned attention to his talk. Then she had thought that every footstep which passed was his, and one that she was sure she knew half stopped,—how her heart beat!—but it passed on, and, a few minutes after, she saw Harry in his place again. It required a strong effort to keep down those rising tears; but the curtain drew up again, and no one but herself knew what had caused that troubled heaving of her bosom a few moments before.

Egerton found the music of the next act particularly soothing to his feelings,—so much so that he left the house before it came to an end.

An hour or two afterwards, Villars was returning from the House of Commons with Grey, who had been eliciting some applause for his maiden speech. The conversation had branched off from politics to the various pursuits and professions which their college friends had entered; and Egerton, among others, had come under discussion.

It was the greatest pity, Grey was saying, that he had got into such a bad set. "That lot of men you see loitering about Long's is about the worst in London for a man to get into. Poor old Harry!" he added, " I'm sorry for him—he used to be a very good fellow."

"But so he is still," Charlie urged, "only that he's such a reckless beggar now, thanks to the set he lives with. They haven't quite succeeded in spoiling him yet."

"Can't touch tar and hope to escape tarnation," Grey replied. "And, talking of black things, isn't that very like his make in front of us?"

They had just turned the corner of St. James's Street, and the individual in question was walking before them in company with a young crossing-sweeper with a broom under his arm.

Quickening their pace, they came up within a yard or two of the pair, and found Egerton engaged in familiar conversation with the barefooted boy, and questioning him upon his earnings as they walked together up St. James's Street.

"You call a shilling a good day, then?" Harry was saying.

Very good indeed, the boy said. Sometimes he didn't get sixpence, and sometimes only a penny. He had had a great day on one occasion, upon the arrival of some distinguished potentate in London; had actually taken three shillings.

"And what did you do with it?" Harry asked.

Bought stock with it. What was stock? Why, pocket-books, pencils, and such-like. A pocket-book was to be had for fourpence halfpenny in London, and sold for a shilling in the country. He could beg a bit of dinner from some house, and sleep where he could. And that's what he'd do now if he could save half-a-crown. But he didn't see how that was ever to be accomplished according to his present rate of earning. "There was some," he said, "as kept crossings to themselves, and took a deal of money. But the police wouldn't allow them chaps to stay on a crossing, took them up for begging, and so they was forced to do the best they could."

In reply to Egerton's further inquiries, he gave him a short account of his early history and antecedents; where he lodged, how he paid a shilling a week rent, and was sixpence in arrear; how his landlady gave him a crust of bread and some tea for his supper; and various other interesting particulars he communicated, which, being given in an ingenuous kind of manner, produced at length the wished-for half-crown. There was a considerable element of generosity in Egerton's liberality, but, on the whole, perhaps it ought to be attributed more to that mere indolent habit of giving which carelessness in regard of money is apt to generate.

The sweeper, however, cared little for the motive. He had his coveted half-crown, and ran off with it in great glee to his distant lodging; and Harry, having prolonged his walk to the top of Bond Street, turned to retrace his steps, and found himself face to face with Villars and Grey, from whom he underwent some little pleasantry on the subject of his newly-made friend. This topic being exhausted, the former asked if Harry was going to this ball, where " everybody " was going?

" No, I'm going to bed," he answered.

"I'm sick of balls." And he relapsed into a moody, monosyllabic state after that, until they arrived at the door of the club, where the others said good night, and left him. But, notwithstanding that he was so utterly *blasé*, an hour or two afterwards Charlie saw him standing at the top of the stairs at this very house.

"Why, I thought you were not coming?" he said.

"I didn't intend to," Egerton answered. "But I didn't feel inclined to go to bed, and so I did, you see."

"So I see," Charlie rejoined, and passed on, wondering what this short answer might mean.

A few moments after he might have been still more surprised to see the cold bow which his sister received from Harry as she passed, and might perhaps have been able to account for her *distrait* manner, and her anxiety to go directly the carriage came.

Miss Grant was the only person Harry had danced with until he heard Lady Mary Villars' carriage announced. But directly he had seen, through the banisters, Blanche and her mother disappear into the night, he commenced dancing most vigorously, talked and laughed with unusual gaiety, rather avoided Charlie, and went away about half-past three, after many glasses of champagne, in company with a couple of other boisterously merry friends.

A Hansom race to Covent Garden was suggested when they got into the street. Three Hansoms are accordingly with difficulty collected, the drivers are made to get inside, and the three ball-goers mount up behind, crack their whips, and forrard away! They rattle up Piccadilly, along Coventry Street and Leicester Square, jeered by passing cabmen, running the gauntlet of giant market carts, shaving the corners of lamp-posts down King Street, shouting, whipping, laughing, and astonishing the old cab horses at their own powers of speed, until they are brought to a stand-still by the waggons of vegetables and other food. They then dismount, and proceed to the inspection of the early market, chaff the stall-keepers, and provoke brilliant repartees from old men from the country,—try the tempers of several old women by depreciating their vegetables, and finally come to an anchor opposite to a flower-stall, and gladden the hearts of several women who are trying to cheapen very cheap bundles of flowers by treating them all round. Laden with fresh strawberries and roses, they remount their cabs, whip the wretched screws back to their several rooms, reward the drivers liberally, and turn in.

Turning in, however, did not, with Egerton, mean going to sleep. In the silence and solitude of his room, all the bitter thoughts, which the forced excitement of the last few hours had only suspended, came rushing back upon his mind. And as he tossed from side to side on his hot and weary pillow, and thought how all the fond schemes in which he had indulged were scattered to the empty air, and how it mattered very little now what became of him, how deep he plunged into reckless dissipation, he was filled with a torturing agony of unrest, which only derived fresh stimulus from the recollection of those tender looks and tones which memory insisted upon bringing up to mock his misery.

The busy world was already in the full career of daily life before a calmer mood set in, and exhausted nature dropped off at last to sleep—and perhaps to dream.

CHAPTER X.

Sunday is not a cheerful day in London. There is an unnatural air of quiet about the streets, a feeling of stagnation which acts with an oppressive effect upon the mind. Everybody seems to go to ground. There is a shut-up-and-gone-away-for-the-day look about the place, which is very depressing to the spirits of any man who has not gone away for the day. The business man may enjoy the cessation from the bustle of the week; but the idle man, whose only business is his pleasure, finds the time hang very heavy on hand when his occupation is thus temporarily suspended. Even sunshine cannot altogether dispel the listless, wearisome feeling which envelops him; and a wet Sunday—don't even allude to the subject, please.

Egerton was an idle man (unless betting can be called an occupation), and Egerton was in London on this Sunday preceding the Derby, and Egerton was weary and depressed.

The day was bright enough without, but there was a dull, heavy cloud casting its gloomy shadow over all his thoughts, and giving a sickly hue to every hope and every interest.

Despondency and apprehension, too, in regard to the race, which in a pecuniary sense was to make or mar him, had now taken the place of former confidence. Something kept telling him now that he should lose; and if he did lose, it was his last throw, and the stakes were heavy, far away beyond any means he ever should possess of paying; there would be nothing for it but to seek a refuge from pursuit in some foreign country, where he should have to drag out a miserable life on perhaps a smaller pittance than his father now allowed him.

Drearily he sat gazing from the window

of the empty club, hugging his torturing thoughts, and brooding over the troubles which he told himself were to come.

Manners' cheerful voice roused him at length, and he looked up with such a melancholy absent interest, that Tom rallied him upon his mood, and asked what was the matter—was he in love?

No, Harry said, with a sort of smile; a little low, that was all.

"Come, cheer up, old boy!" cried Manners. "It'll never do to go along so, Mr. Brown. What do you say to church? Have you been?"

"Oh! blow Wells Street," was Manners' rejoinder, when Egerton said that he would go there with him if he liked; he was rather in the humour for good music. "There's always such a devil of a crowd there, and so infernally hot. I'll take you to a deuced good man, not far from here. Short service and good sermon—stirs one up, you know. You don't want to argue, I suppose?" And in order that he might have no opportunity for so doing, Manners took his arm and walked him off without further ceremony.

If Harry had been at all disposed for arguing, he might, perhaps, have had a good deal to say in favour of good music *versus* sermon. He might have said that he hardly ever heard a sermon which produced anything like the solemn feelings of devotion which thrilled through him sometimes as he listened to the grand peal of the organ, or the bursts of praise and rapture from the 'full-voiced quire below,' which found so ready an echo in his inmost soul, and purified and exalted for the time his thoughts.

Many people will tell you that the desire for good music in church betokens a false religion—a religion of the senses. And they set down music as a fringe of divine worship, in company with the elaborate decorations and sensational ornament which appeal to the eye only, and which, in churches like those of Margaret Street and Wells Street, are calculated to revolt the mind rather than to impress it. Who can help feeling indignation at the sight of an altar got up with parti-coloured cloths and costly finery, and the approaches to it filled with brilliant flowers and plants, as if it were the entrance to a ball-room? But, granted that the emotions which music produces are very often transient—is it in the power of many preachers to produce even a transient impression?

Then these people tell you that you must have very little real religion, if you require to have it assisted by adventitious aids. But then the majority of us have very little real religion. We are not all so well equipped with good desires and solemn thoughts as to be able to summon up feelings of devotion at any time and in any place. And, therefore, if ill-read prayers and worse-delivered sermons have not the effect of inducing religious feelings, it is surely well to go where good impressions may be produced upon the heart, even if they should come through the gutter of the senses. Gabbled prayers, and prosy, monotonous, cold-drawn sermons are apt to produce feelings of irritation rather than of religion. Teach our spiritual advisers that, even without great talent or eloquence, the attention may be fixed and the mind influenced, and then it will not be necessary to hunt after churches where the service will be at least impressively performed.

The clergyman whom Manners had substituted for Egerton's music on the present occasion was an exception to the general run of pulpit ecclesiastics. He read the prayers as if he were praying, and his preaching was neither a string of trite Scripture phrases, which fell with a meaningless sound upon the ear; nor was it merely a florid exhibition of eloquence, which aroused an admiration for the man rather than for the truths he advocated. It was a sermon with which the greatest stickler for doctrinal exercises in the pulpit could have found no fault; and yet it was full of sound practical lessons for every-day life, enforced with a deep earnestness of manner and warmth of language which burned conviction into the heart. His theology was a theology of broad human interest, not a narrow tilting-ground for the rival dogmas of a sect. He preached religion, but he illustrated, explained, and pointed out the application of what he preached. And though enjoining with all the eloquence at his command a deep love and reverence for the Bible and the teaching which it contained, he yet denounced with the strongest censure the fallacy of that pietistic theory of life which clergymen are in the habit of dwelling upon. Many, probably, from having but a limited range of thought; the majority, perhaps, from never thinking at all.

He showed clearly how impossible it was to separate natural from revealed religion, or to disconnect the Christian system of morality from the Bible law upon which it was founded. Their morality, he told them, was ennobled by the motives which the Bible supplied. Every act of their lives, when sanctified by the motive, was an act of religion. The performance of a Christian's moral obligations, the fulfilment of his human duties—this was his religion. It was the most mischievous error to suppose that a religious life was a life of prayer only,—that morality, so called, was outside the department of a religious person. It was possible to have a morality founded on instinct, as the heathens had; but without the motives which the Christian religion supplied, such a morality was dead and worthless. To neglect morality for the sake of religion was little short of infatuation. A life spent in the service of God did not mean a life spent in the neglect of man. To do God's will upon earth was the object for which every human being had been sent into the world. God's will was the happiness of man. And, therefore, it was the duty of every man to contribute, as far as in him lay, towards the promotion of that end. For this purpose faculties and powers in greater or less degree had been granted to every man, and according as they were used, so would he be judged. A life spent in merely selfish devotion was a life misspent, a life of wasted opportunities, a life of faculties and gifts misused or unemployed. Let a man do his duty in the station of life or profession in which he had been placed, and God would be much better pleased than if he neglected his human duties for a life of barren asceticism and seclusion. It was in the power of everyone, no matter how circumstanced, to add something to the general stock of human happiness. If a man had no field for active exertion open to him, he could still cultivate that gentleness and forbearance and self-forgetfulness which should increase the comfort or the pleasure of those with whom he came in contact—he could always so regulate and improve his own character that others around him might be insensibly influenced for good by the impression which he unwittingly caused. And thus the great end which all men should have in view, it was in the power of all men to promote.

There was another evil, he said, which sprang from this separation of religion from the ordinary life of the world. It was by this means made to appear something so dull and gloomy and distasteful, that many were deterred from approaching the subject at all. It might seem an audacious paradox to assert that it was to religion of this kind that much of the irreligion and immorality of society were due; but the assertion, he believed, would not be more bold than true. The persons who advocated these mistaken views set a ban upon all innocent amusement, and refused to enjoy the goods which were given them to be enjoyed. They went about with a gloomy countenance, tabooed the harmless pleasures of youth, and turned a sour eye upon all merriment and mirth, as if God had not given us the power of such enjoyment to minister to our delight as much as any other of the manifold senses and perceptions with which we had been endowed. By such a misrepresentation did they so traduce religion, that they practically invited men to avoid a knowledge of what far higher attractions were possessed by the pleasures which it did sanction, than could be claimed by those gross excitements which it did not sanction.

"The really religious man," he said, in conclusion, "the man who makes a good use of his time upon earth, who does not fritter away his life in frivolous amusement, or in unserviceable devotion; but who, while endeavouring faithfully to know and to perform his duty in this world, is looking forward to a bright future in a world beyond; who enjoys the consciousness of a life devoted to the service of his fellow-creatures, and an earnest desire to employ to their utmost the faculties with which he has been intrusted; who feels that his Creator is present to his every thought and every action; who sees Him in all His works—in earth, and sea, and sky; in summer landscape and in winter storm; in tree and flower; in murmuring stream and raging sea—such a man is imbued with a deep pervading cheerfulness with which no exotic mirth, no earth-born happiness can compare. Though this earth be now crumbling to decay, though England be soon tossed among the fragments of a broken world, though even now the hidden fires of the globe be gathering strength to blast this mighty product of Almighty power,—what matters it to that man who is persevering in his duty to his God and to his neighbour? His hope is steadfast, his immortality secure. The terrors of that final doom when time shall be no more, when the fiery bonds of the universe shall crack and part, and earth shrivel up like a parched scroll, shall come upon him undismayed. Upborne upon the steady wings of faith, he shall soar above the jarring discord of this ruined world, and enter for all eternity into the glory of the everlasting God. Strive to obtain that wisdom from above which shall direct you in the way to this calm and holy confidence, which shall teach you to free yourselves from earth while yet upon the earth, which shall show you the worthlessness of this world's pleasures, which pall and satisfy so soon. And when at last death shall lay his chilly hand upon your earthly frame, when the joys and friendships which attracted you in this transient life are dimly fading from your view, what bliss unutterable shall be yours when the vision of coming glory breaks upon your raptured gaze, when heaven's wide portals are opened to receive your parting spirit; and when, amid the jubilees of angels and archangels around His glorious throne, He shall say to you, before the myriad brightness of rejoicing heaven, 'Well done, thou good and faithful servant, enter thou into thy Master's joy!'"

A glow of enthusiasm lighted up the preacher's face as he concluded, and there was a still and solemn silence as he closed his Bible, paused a moment, and then impressively dismissed the congregation.

"Well, what did you think of my sermon, Harry?" asked Manners, as they walked up the street.

Egerton admitted that the experiment had been a success. "You know," he continued presently, "I believe, if you come to think of it, one does lead a very useless life. I'm not conscious of ever having been of any use in the world; are you?"

"Well, I don't know that I have," Manners answered, carelessly. "I manage to enjoy life though, somehow."

Harry mused. He was thinking, perhaps, of his life for the last few months, and wondering whether one single thought or act would bear looking into. And he determined at this moment that, after the Derby, he wouldn't make another bet. He would do something, at least, which should lift him out of the mire in which he felt that he was now sunk. If he didn't lose, that was to say, and there was the rub.

Manners' more mercurial nature delighted not to dwell for long on serious thoughts. "What's the odds, as long as you're happy?" was his principle. And after they had walked on in silence for some minutes, he asked where they were going, and suggested the Zoo; and when Egerton demurred, on the plea that they would see nobody there whom they knew, he said, "Come down to Richmond, then. I'll give you a dinner; and the country air will pick you up a bit, old boy; you're not yourself to-day."

Egerton was agreeable. The afternoon was bright; the change would be pleasant; and a Hansom, therefore, was summoned, and directed to pilot them to that resort of Sunday diners.

The air was fresh, the lanes were cool and

green, and therefore it mattered little that their horse was slow. It was nearly seven o'clock before they stood on the terrace of the "Star and Garter," and looked down upon the wide view which presented so charming a contrast to vistas of glaring pavements and endless chimneys, streets, and railings. Far away below into the clear distance stretched a luxurious plain of green foliage, out of which there peeped at intervals the white walls of nestling villa or tidy farm. The stately Thames gleamed like a golden plateau in the rays of the declining sun, winding up into woodland shades, where the imagination conjured up sweet flowery meads and drooping ferns and smooth green leafy glades along its course; the outriggers which skimmed across its surface seeming from above like spiders upon the calm waters of an evening lake, and that giant barge, which glided through their midst, like some uncouth Triton among the glancing minnows. The evening breeze bore upward the delicious perfume of the new-mown hay, and fanned the cheeks with a country freshness all its own. The birds from that shady grove give their joyous music to the ear, and the clouds which float about the dying sun are tinged with the lustre of his golden light. The only thing to mar complete enjoyment is the consciousness of a crowd, the sound of boisterous laughter, and a half-caught clatter of knives and forks behind.

Dinner discussed, and Harry's spirits a little the better for the generous vintage of Champagne, they adjourn to the terrace again.

Night has already fallen upon the scene; lights gleam from the windows; parties are hurrying off to the train, and they have the place almost to themselves.

The crescent moon is rising in the distant sky, the far-off woods are chequered with her shadowy ray, the broad river stretches away below in glittering curves of light, 'the great stars globe themselves in heaven,' and the soft night air scarce dissipates the curling smoke from their cigars, as it mingles with the scent of garden flowers and sweet-smelling shrubs.

There was a calm for even a despairing heart at such a time; but it was a calm, Harry thought, which only preceded the coming storm. Dull, heavy, lowering, the dark cloud still hung before him and marred his peace, and a weight still pressed upon his thoughts, which no repose could hope to lift, or change of scene relieve; yet there was a lull from the racking pain which had worn him for the last few days, and for even this small respite he was thankful. No forgetfulness, though, nor would there be; and he sighed a heavy sigh.

"Why that sigh, old boy?" asked Manners, removing his cigar from his lips, and turning to Harry. "What's the matter with you to-day? Been losing lately, or what?"

Not more than usual, Egerton said, as if he was so accustomed to it now, that that didn't affect him. It was his way, he said, to feel low occasionally.

Had he not made it up with his father yet? Manners asked. Why did he not go and represent to him that this state of things really could not be allowed to go on any longer, that the joke had been carried quite far enough, and that he should be obliged to him now if he would take another line; in fact, that he (Harry) must insist upon his doing so.

Harry smiled as he said that it was possible his father might be obtuse enough not to see the force of his representations.

"Try another tack, then," Manners suggested. "Put it to him feelingly. Say how it grieves you to see an old and respectable gentleman behaving in such a misguided way; that a tender interest and concern for his character have compelled you, much against your inclination, to sacrifice your own private feelings for his benefit; and that you have felt it to be your duty to point out to him—eh? to point out to him —-the error of his ways, and to awaken him to a sense of the propriety which—which it is so much his interest to——; in fact, that he had better come down at once."

"Broke down in the straight, Tom!" cried Harry, laughing. "The pace at the beginning killed you. Never mind, you'll do for the House some day."

" 'Pon my soul, I believe so!" laughed Manners. " I'm sure I could talk as good bosh as some of 'em. What do you think?"

" By the way, wasn't Charlie Villars standing for some place the other day?" he continued, breaking away from his point. " Got beaten, didn't he?"

" He was only canvassing for Grey," Harry said; and Manners, who, until the last few days, had been in the wilds of Scotland fishing, went on to say that he had also heard that Charlie was now a great man in London.

" Lady Dufton has taken him up rather," Egerton said. " He led a cotillon there the other night."

" You don't mean to say he's come to that? A man must be very far gone when he takes to leading cotillons, eh?"

Harry only half understood what Manners had said. The mention of his friend had called up other thoughts; and he answered absently that Villars had not absolutely become a lady's hack yet. He didn't think he would; he had too much in him for that.

"They tell me," Manners said, "that there were great games going on at Lady Dufton's the other night." And he proceeded to discuss with much relish some of the piquant stories which were told of Lady Dufton and other ladies of similarly easy virtue.

Egerton was able to contribute a few interesting particulars which had come under his own observation; and being in a moralising humour (even gay young men will moralise sometimes), he said that he thought all that kind of thing very bad.

"I believe," he said, "women only marry now that they may flirt with decency. There's not one of those women that hasn't some man dangling after her; and their husbands don't seem to mind in the least."

"I should take precious good care that my wife knew how to behave herself, if I were married," Manners said. "A man, of course, may do what he likes; but I shouldn't allow Mrs. M. to be kicking and breaking the traces as she pleased."

This was a comfortable male doctrine to which Egerton did not altogether subscribe. But he didn't think it worth arguing, and continued to animadvert upon Lady Dufton's proceedings.

"The odd thing is," he said, "that no one seems to think any the worse of her. One always supposed that any woman who goes on in the way she does would be cut. But it's rather the contrary."

"Well, hang it," Manners replied, with a charming consistency, "I always think it's devilish hard that people should be down upon women so, when men may do just as they like, and nobody minds."

Well, it did seem unfair. But though Egerton was all for women behaving themselves with decency, he didn't know that the instinct which made immodesty in women so much more repugnant to the mind was due to the idea that modesty and purity were more particularly the virtues of women, just as courage was of man.

A coward would be just as much scouted among men as an immodest woman among those of her own sex; and women would despise the coward as much as men do the *traviata*. Both from the same cause: that the objects of their disgust had been untrue to the first qualities of their nature.

Egerton was so very strong upon the point of female transgressions in this respect, that Manners laughingly interrupted him, and told him that he had become quite a moral young man. "You'll be lecturing at some godly institution soon," he said, much tickled at the notion: "a reformatory—refuge—what-do-you-call-'em?—home?"

"You shall have a reserved seat for nothing when I do," rejoined Harry. "But without being a Mrs. Grundy, you know," he continued, "I think society is going to grief rather. Other people follow the example of these women, and think it's the proper thing to do. Old George IV. would feel quite at home, I expect, if he were to come to life again now."

"What a jolly time that must have been!"

laughed Manners; and Harry laughed, too, at the way in which he looked at it.

"Why don't you marry, Tom?" he asked abruptly, after a pause of some moments.

"Marry!" exclaimed Manners, "not if I know it. I'm very happy as I am. Besides, I haven't anything to marry on."

"Your father would give you whatever you wanted."

"Not enough to keep a wife on; they expect such a deuce of a lot of luxury nowadays. Besides, a bachelor's life is much the jollier of the two."

"I don't know that," Harry said, in so low a tone as almost to be inaudible.

"You're surely not thinking of it?" Tom exclaimed. "Don't, now; you'll repent it. And now that I think of it, you used to be rather sweet upon Charlie Villars' sister last year. Is that all off?"

It was not the nudge of Manners' elbow that caused Harry to wince as he did; some momentary spasm, perhaps.

He laughed a short laugh, which, in the

moonlight, had a most sickly effect, and turning the conversation to the Derby, was soon deep in previous running, staying power, make, and speed of various horses,—which interesting subject lasted until they re-entered their Hansom, and drove back through the silent night to the metropolis.

CHAPTER XI.

That it was the Derby week was very evident next day in London. The captain was again upon the town; Piccadilly was redolent of Aldershott and country quarters; every lodging-house was filled in every available corner, and Tattersall's crammed to the doorways as Egerton made his way in there to compare bets before the Epsom meeting commenced.

This lengthy process having been concluded, and one or two more bets added to an already heavy book, he turned his steps in the direction of Curzon Street, with a view to calling upon Maud Farringford, who, with her lord, had returned to town a few days before.

When the first ardour of her delight at seeing him again had passed off, and when their innumerable common interests had been pretty well exhausted, Harry introduced his beggared cousin to her compassion, and asked her to make her mother a medium of communication to Mr. Egerton on his behalf.

Maud would certainly do all she could to further his interests.

"But why not get Philip to do something, Harry dear?" she asked, not thinking what she was saying.

Harry was not very sanguine of assistance in that quarter, and while he was replying to that effect, Maud's husband entered the room.

She ran up to him, and took his arm with a pretty, playful affection, and looked up into his face with a most loving rapture as she told him that Harry had promised to dine with them that evening, adding, "So you mustn't go away, you naughty man, as you did last night."

The handsome but vacant face of the naughty man looked down upon his blooming bride with a very tender interest, as he held out his hand to Harry, and said he should be delighted to see him. He was going to the Derby, of course?

"Oh, you may be sure he is!" exclaimed Maud. "He's always at races,—nearly as often as you are;" and again some mildly abusive epithet was applied to the naughty man, on whose arm she was hanging so lovingly with clasped hands.

A delicious embrace follows, and Harry begins to feel rather sorry that he had said he would dine, if this sort of thing is to go on all through dinner. For it certainly is not much fun being umpire to a newly-married pair, who do nothing but make eyes at each other, and indulge in a constant stream of playful banter, appealing to you, every now and then (the lady particularly), to decide whether it wasn't too cruel of him, or whether he isn't a stupid old dear, or too provoking, or something else—which, if you are to judge from the loving looks with which they regard the culprit, they don't in the least wish you to believe. Some old Greek sage (I'm not sure that it wasn't one of the seven) was similarly bored in his day, and has moralised upon this subject for the benefit of posterity without the slightest effect apparently. All these little points might so very well be settled beforehand up-stairs, and then one would be spared the disagreeable feeling of being *de trop*.

However, Harry dined there, and the next day went down to Epsom on Farringford's drag—while Maud was trying to persuade Philip, who had come up to town for the day, to take an interest in the misfortunes of his cousin.

Philip said that he was extremely sorry for the man; but, really, he didn't see how he could be expected to give him money, when, as far as he knew, he had never had the pleasure of his acquaintance.

"But think," said Maud, "of the poor creature in such distress—almost starving, Harry says. And your own cousin, too; I'm sure you ought to do something for him."

"I suppose it was his own fault that he came to what he is," rejoined Philip. "And really, I haven't money to throw away on every rascal who wants means to gratify his extravagance. Henry had better look after him—they're birds of a feather."

"How can you say such a thing, Philip?" cried Maud, indignantly. "Harry's the kindest, most good-natured creature living. I'm sure I wish you were half as good!"

"I wish I was, indeed!" answered Philip, sarcastically. "He is, no doubt, a most exemplary member of the family,—never gambles, never imposes upon his tradesmen, or cheats his unfortunate creditors. Really, a most admirable young man! quite a pattern gentleman!"

"You may sneer as much as you please," said Maud, the angry tears swelling into her eyes; "but if you had been as badly treated as poor Harry, I dare say you'd have been a great deal worse."

"Oh! he has been shockingly treated, I admit. My father's a perfect monster, and Henry a poor innocent lamb. I'm glad there is somebody who can appreciate the hardship of his case. I dare say his friend at Bethnal Green, or wherever he is, may be able to give him some very useful information how to spend money that he has not got quicker than he is doing at present." Mr. Philip Egerton here rose, with the intention of putting an end to the conversation.

"Philip, I hate you," Maud exclaimed, vehemently, as he moved towards the door. And Philip smiled so sweetly on her as he replied that she did him too much honour, and shut the door behind him.

"What an odious wretch!" thought Maud, "to talk of Harry in that way—his brother, too! Can they be brothers?" And her mother, entering the room at the moment, was treated to a *réchauffé* of her interview with Philip, and desired to interest herself with Mr. Egerton according to Harry's request.

CHAPTER XII.

Drags, omnibuses, waggonets, Hansoms, and every species of blue-veiled vehicle are pouring down Grosvenor Place, Epsomwards. It is the Derby-day. "Uprouse ye then, my merry, merry men, it is the Derby-day." Have not thousands throughout the United Kingdom been looking forward for months to this day, which is to be the ruin or the making of many, and shall we sit unconcernedly at home when the town is at Epsom? Hardly. We have promised to go down with Harry Egerton, and we meet him accordingly at Victoria Station. The previous day, he tells us, was not a good one for backers, but he came off about quits; and if the favourite only wins to day, by Jove! we shall have no end of a dinner at any place we like to name.

But Harry does not appear to contemplate the event with that calm confidence which would make us look upon our dinner as a certainty. He has evidently had a restless night, and his careless joviality of demeanour, to close observers like ourselves, is clearly put on. It is only natural that he should be nervous and excited; but besides the uncertainty of winning or losing, there is an undercurrent of anxiety which makes a swirl upon the surface occasionally, and ruffles any evenness of thought which might exist.

Running his eye over the *Morning Post* before starting, the following announcement had attracted his attention, and scarcely acted as a sedative to his feelings:—"We are informed that a marriage has been arranged between the Marquis of Galston and Miss Villars, only daughter of Mr. and Lady Mary Villars."

This was not a pleasant paragraph to come across at such a time, and Harry had clenched his hands, and almost bitten his lip through (after the manner of Guy Livingstone), as he read it; thought that he would just as soon lose as win now, and had gone down to the station despondent and depressed. Our genial companionship has recalled him to the real interest of the day; and by the time he has arrived on the course, forced himself up the stairs into the stand, and fought his way into the enclosure, Blanche Villars is forgotten for the time being in the all-absorbing excitement of the place,—cropping up, though, every now and then to give him a twinge between the races, and not altogether laid by copious draughts of champagne at luncheon.

The course is being cleared. The roar of the book-makers is at its height—the sea of faces is disposing itself to inspect the preliminary canter—there is not an inch of space unoccupied on the top of the stand—line upon line and row upon row of drags and carriages are covered with men and women up to Tattenham Corner—the hill is alive with humanity—the boxes in the stand are filled with gay toilettes, and everywhere pale faces are anxiously expecting the appearance of their favourite. One by one they issue from the paddock, parade in a long line before the multitude, and after the usual spin to stretch their muscles, assemble at the post.

Minute after minute goes by, and they are not off yet! The suspense was terrible—the favourite was restive, and would break away! But at last there's a roar from the top of the stand, the bugle sounds, and the start for the Derby has been accomplished.

Watch them now flying along the top of the hill; now see them sweeping round Tattenham Corner; strain your eyes, Harry Egerton, to descry the favourite's colours, and with horror on your face, and a sinking in your heart, see his jockey already riding him while yet fifty lengths or more from the post! See them shoot past, and the favourite drop behind, and tell us what your feelings were when the numbers showed an outsider as the winner, and the favourite not even placed!

The crash, then, had come at last. He had lost more than almost any run of luck would enable him to pay. The book-makers knew that he and many others were " gone," and those whom he met on his way out looked very curiously at him, he thought, as he brushed past. He had no heart to stay any longer upon the course; and so he joined the crowd and the excitement and the noise which were streaming towards the station again—taking no notice of anybody or anything, but wandering on mechanically, utterly prostrated and sick at heart.

Manners recognises him in the crowd, and persuades him to come back on his drag, which was to start at once. Harry reluctantly acquiesces. He would sooner have been alone; but he had not energy to refuse. And Manners, knowing that he had lost heavily, tried to cheer him up, kindly enough, but to little purpose. There were others on that drag whose gloomy faces told of heavy hearts within, and it was a very, very forced gaiety which even a deluge of champagne was able to produce. But none were so hopelessly involved, none had plunged so deeply and so recklessly as Egerton; and what fitful and spasmodic interest he had been able to evince in the conversation around him had flickered and died away long before they reached London.

As they drove up between the lines of carriages and people in Grosvenor Place, Villars, who had returned by train, espied from a balcony his dejected face and attitude—saw and pitied—left the house and followed Harry to his rooms. There, away from the distractions of the road, the rallying of friends, and the tumult of sounds which had before surrounded him, his position had come upon him with a terrible reality and force, and he was sitting—unwashed, dusty, just as he had thrown himself down—the picture of hopeless, utter despair.

"Harry, my dear old boy!" cried Villars, coming up to him and taking the hand which, feebly smiling, he held out, "I'm so very sorry for you! Have you lost much?"

"A good deal more, Charlie, than I can ever pay."

"But can't I help you? Do let me lend you some money, or do something for you."

"My *dear* Charlie," Harry answered,

looking up at him gratefully, "you couldn't, I'm afraid. I'm over four thousand to the bad."

No wonder Charlie's breath was taken away for an instant.

"How could you possibly stand to lose that?" he asked.

"I suppose I was a fool—a blackguard, if you like. But I thought that devil *must* win."

The fortitude with which he had borne his previous losses had utterly deserted him now. There was no longer the Derby to look forward to, to pull it all back. And what he was to do, Heaven only knew! He might win a few hundreds on the Oaks; but what good would they be? He couldn't put off the ring men any more. He should be posted at Tattersall's—not able to show his face on any race-course, or at all events in the ring. Duns, whom he had staved off till after this race, would all come down upon him again now; and, as if one more drop was required to add to the bitterness of his cup, the only girl he had ever really cared about, for whom he thought now that he could almost have died, if required, so passionately did he love her, now that she was out of his reach,—that she should be engaged to another man! why, in the face of this overwhelming accumulation of troubles, should he continue to live? Life could no longer have enjoyment for him, surrounded as he was by difficulty, despair, anxiety, and gnawing jealousy, and love which was denied him. And dark thoughts were forcing their way into his mind when Charlie entered the room.

With the morning, however, came calmer feelings. Not that there was much relief in the dull, heavy depression which had settled itself upon his spirits; but when he came to think that there were many of his friends in the same position as himself, it was some little consolation. One or two, he found, had already gone abroad. Should he go over to the Continent for a time? No money! Borrow? Sick of borrowing! What, then, was he to do? He couldn't have the face to ask anyone to back a bill for him for the amount he required. Go to his father? Should he go to his father, and make one more appeal to his compassion? Was it likely, when he refused to pay a small sum, that he would pay nearly ten times the amount now? Hardly likely. Propose to Miss Grant, heiress? Could he do that? Could he? And he fell into a train of troubled reflection, which ended with—No, by Jove! not till everything else fails. And then Lady Belvedere came upon the scene. Would she, perhaps, help him if he told her what a strait he was in? It was worth trying. He could hint it gently first, and if that didn't succeed, boldly disclose the whole business, and ask her to do something for him. Something must be done, and there seemed nothing else for it. So, after another day and night of restless thought, he pays the proposed visit to his rich and good-natured aunt.

It is a question, perhaps, whether her good-nature would have stood the trial to which he proposed to submit it, had the opportunity been afforded to him. But it was not; for he found her in such a state of nervous agitation, that the introduction of the subject at all was out of the question. Lady Belvedere, indeed, had given orders that no one was to be admitted; but the servant had made an exception in favour of Mr. Henry Egerton, who was known to be a favourite nephew. And he had found her lying on the sofa in a semi-hysterical condition, with her smelling-bottle in her hand, and an open letter lying on the table by her side.

In reply to Harry's inquiries, she informed him, in excited tones, that she had received that morning a letter containing the strangest and most unexpected intelligence. All these long years she had lived in the belief that her only child had died when quite a baby; and now she receives a letter which obscurely hints at the probability of his being still alive; where, or in what circumstances, the writer cannot say. This letter had been written to prepare her for the fact. Further explanation would follow in due course, she was told. There was no address or signature; but the handwriting was a foreigner's.

Wasn't it enough to upset anybody's nerves? Lady Belvedere asked, as she again applied to her smelling-bottle.

It certainly was, Harry thought. Though, indeed, there did not seem to be any very sufficient reason for the excitement and interest which the intelligence seemed to have caused to himself. "Was there no clue given?" he asked eagerly. And his hand almost trembled as he took the letter, at Lady Belvedere's suggestion, and read it over again to her.

None whatever! They might indulge in the wildest conjectures. The only sort of hint was to be found in the handwriting; and that might mean anything or nothing. Perhaps it was a hoax; some clever imposture for the purpose of obtaining money out of her ladyship. But then, as she said, it would be such a strange thing to enter into anybody's head. And the writer evidently knew every particular of the period of her life when her child was supposed to have died.

The more Lady Belvedere thought about it, the more nervous and agitated she became; and she was obliged at last to get Harry to sit down and write a note to her doctor, to come and prescribe a sedative.

All thought of pecuniary difficulties had flown from Harry's mind as he left his aunt's house. It seemed to him as if this strange news had not come unexpectedly upon him. It was no hoax; he was persuaded of that. There would be a disclosure, he knew—and what? He seemed to be walking on air for a few moments. There would be a Lord Belvedere, then, and a great deal of the property which Lady Belvedere now held would be his. What use would the new Lord Belvedere make of his property? How people in London would talk about it! What strange things did happen sometimes in the world, and what a cruel suspense Lady Belvedere was being condemned to until the next letter arrived! He could sympathise with her most sincerely. There was such a reality about his sympathy, too, that for the whole of that day he was unable to fix his attention on any subject, and passed the night in a state of restless inquietude and most extravagantly curious dreams.

CHAPTER XIII.

SATURDAY and Sunday (and many following days) passed without any further light being thrown upon Lady Belvedere's letter; and Harry was obliged to turn his thoughts again to the heavy settlement which had to be made on the very next day.

It was all very well for him to try and put a good face upon it, and to make merry at his own expense, and joke about his losses with others who had been hard hit, like himself. He would, in such company, talk of turning book-maker—investing in cigar lights—box of lights, cigar lights.

"What do you think of the touting business?" he asked of Skindles. "Don't you think one might turn an honest penny by that?"

Skindles had a natural preference for the

three-card trick, at which he was already an expert. And Harry finally decided that he should lay out his last shilling in a broom —"You ought to get a first-rate broom for a bob, oughtn't you?"—and sweep the crossing in front of his father's door.

But this assumed gaiety, which familiarity with his losses now allowed of, gave way to increasing perplexity and apprehension as the settling day approached. And again he twisted and tortured his mind to devise some expedient for meeting his liabilities or for compassing a temporary delay.

In the present state of his aunt's mind it would hardly be decent to intrude his affairs upon her; that outlet, therefore, was closed up. After all, there seemed to be nothing for it but to apply to his father. He could not well lose anything by it; he couldn't be worse off than he was; and it might succeed. It should be done. Hopeless though it seemed, and disagreeable and humiliating though it would be, it was his only chance.

Accordingly, after an earlier breakfast than

usual, he braced up his nerves next morning to go through the ordeal, and might have been seen, about the hour of eleven o'clock, walking slowly down in the direction of Eaton Place, with rather a pale face, and a step which grew more and more hesitating the nearer he approached to his father's door.

Mr. Egerton was in his study, the footman said; and Harry desired the servant to announce him at once, without asking permission.

He tried very hard to walk firmly and to appear at his ease as the door opened, and he was ushered once more into his father's presence. But he was conscious of a very quick pulsation of the heart, a rather trembling hold upon his hat, and an unpleasant dryness about the mouth, which promised ill for the success of his cause.

Mr. Egerton was at that moment engaged upon a letter to his lawyer on the subject of his starving relation; although, when Mrs. Greville had mentioned the subject to him, and told him her authority, he had said that he didn't believe a word of it—that the man had been dead some years. He was nevertheless giving his lawyer instructions to make inquiries about him when Mr. Henry was announced.

Mr. Henry's father visibly started at the name. But he checked at once the impulse of affection which prompted him to receive his erring son with open arms, and formed his face into an expression of angry coldness instead: anger towards the servant for having shown him in; surprise, anger, and coldness at Harry's intrusion.

The latter read the feeling in his face, as he hesitatingly advanced into the room; and finding that no hand was outstretched to welcome him, was about to explain the reason of his visit, when Mr. Egerton, laying down his pen, demanded why he had forced himself into his presence again.

"I thought," he added, "that I was sufficiently explicit at our last interview?"

"You were, father," was the reply. "And I should not have attempted to see you again, as you didn't wish it" (his voice trembled a little), "if I had not been driven to it by necessity."

Mr. Egerton had felt strongly inclined at first to forget the past, and hold out his hand in token of reconciliation. But the mention of the word necessity recalled him to himself again. The softened expression faded from his eye; and he was again the stern, consistent parent,—natural instinct nobly sacrificed to an overpowering sense of duty.

"I told you," he answered, "on the last occasion on which I held any communication with you on the subject of your debts, that I should take no notice whatever of any applications made to me for payment. To that I have nothing further to add."

"But what *am* I to do, father?" Harry urged, appealingly. "How am I ever to pay them? You give me no chance. I want to live quietly and economically, but you make me reckless by driving me to the wall in this way!"

"From what I hear of your proceedings during the last year," Mr. Egerton replied,

"I am only confirmed in my opinion that the course which I took was the only one open to me to adopt. If I had seen any wish to retrench the extravagance you have been indulging in, I might, perhaps, have thought otherwise. But what do I hear? That you are to be seen at every race meeting, that you are throwing your money about (wherever you get it from) as if you were a prince instead of a younger son with no expectations; and you wish me to provide you with more money to squander as before. But I shall not do it, and therefore——"

"I solemnly declare," broke in the son, "that it was only the absolute want of money that drove me back into betting again. If my debts had been paid, I intended, and would have avoided ever asking you to pay them for me again,—asking you to pay anything over my allowance."

"I don't believe it; you have shown no evidence of such an intention." And Mr. Egerton, feeling that he was forcing himself to harsh language, against which his heart rebelled, continued in the same vein of false argument which Harry had just refuted.

"If I had seen you endeavouring to do something for yourself," he said, "instead of spending your time in gambling and idleness, it would have been a very different thing,—a very different thing!"

"But what could I possibly do?" rejoined Harry. "I was forced into gambling to get money. And now I've lost so much that it's more than ever out of my power to pay."

"You've lost more money!" exclaimed his father, with contracted brow. "You come to ask me to pay more gambling debts! Why, I'm surprised at your impudence!"

"I must get money somehow, and you'll only make me do something desperate, if you won't help me in any way."

"If my son chooses to be a profligate and a spendthrift, sir, it is immaterial to me what becomes of him."

"No, it isn't, father; you know it isn't!" cried Harry, passionately, approaching nearer to the table. "You know you wouldn't like to see me forced into dishonesty, or starving in the streets, perhaps. You don't want to make a blackguard of me, do you?"

Mr. Egerton, in spite of him, winced as he listened to his son's appeal to the affection which he found it so hard to suppress. And his face for a moment or two was working with a mixture of feelings which it required a strong effort to control. But he did it, and answered with a would-be firmness—

"It's of no use pursuing the matter further,—what I have said, I mean to adhere to; and you need expect nothing further from me than what you already receive— which, indeed, is far more than you deserve."

Harry drew himself up. "Then you refuse positively to give me any help whatever?"

Mr. Egerton bowed his head decisively.

"Then I hope, father, that God may forgive you; and that you may not, some day, be sorry for the way you are treating me now. Good-bye," he said, in a low voice, as he opened the door; "I shall not trouble you again."

Mr. Egerton listened to his retreating steps, heard the hall door close with a heavy, reproachful sound, and then sank back, deadly pale, in his chair. The effort of controlling his emotions and the revulsion of feeling had been too much for him,—he was dead!

CHAPTER XIV.

ALL unconsciously, Harry wanders thoughtfully and sadly down the street. He was touched, rather than angry, at his father's unrelenting mood; and for the present the sentimental rather than the practical bearing of his position was uppermost in his mind.

His last card had been played with no effect. Settling was out of the question—what was he now to do? His excited interest in Lady Belvedere's mysterious communication, which the immediate pressure for money had set aside for the time, again asserted itself, and once more he turned his steps in the direction of her house. If all that should come to nothing (and he was despondent now), there was one last resource. It didn't so much matter now if he did adopt it. It was better than living in this kind of way. So perhaps it was as well, after all, that Blanche was gone. 'Ah! Blanche, I thought better of you,' he said to himself, with a weary sigh, as he crossed over on to the pavement of Piccadilly, and lapsed for relief into the contemplation of another side of his misery, thinking for the hundredth time or more that the world could not contain a creature more thoroughly persecuted and wretched than himself.

His thoughts were interrupted by a voice behind him, saying in lugubrious tones evidently intended for his ear. "'And Melancholy marked him for her own.'"

The speaker was Grey, who continued as he came up and took Egerton's arm—

"'My pensive *Harry*, wherefore look you sad?
I had a grandmother, she kept a donkey
To carry to the mart her crockery ware,
And when that donkey looked me in the face,
His face was sad, and you are sad, my *Harry*.'"

Egerton laughed, or tried to laugh. Was he sad? Perhaps he was. The cares of life were beginning to press upon him. He almost wished he was in Parliament, that he might have nothing to think about.

Grey took him to task for his cynical views of youthful legislators. And perhaps, in his case, the remark did not apply; for Grey had a sort of notion that there was some kind of responsibility connected with the position of a member of Parliament. In fact, Egerton used to say that he always shook hands with you now as if you were a constituent.

His remarks, however, were cut short very soon by Galston, who stopped for a moment to speak to Grey, while Harry moved on impatiently, after a slight recognition.

It was some little relief to his feelings to throw off his dislike to Grey, when he rejoined him; and the latter agreed with him partly. But as he didn't see very much of his lordship, they had had no opportunity of quarrelling.

"He's going abroad," Grey continued. "I don't think he takes kindly to his refusal."

"What refusal?"

"Didn't you know he wanted to marry Miss Villars, and she wouldn't have anything to say to him?"

"She refused him!" cried Harry, standing still, and looking eagerly at his companion.

"Why so excited?" asked Grey, in some surprise. And as Harry resumed his walk, he continued, "I thought everybody knew that. They say she wanted to marry somebody else."

Who that somebody else was, Grey had not cared to inquire; and not having been in London the previous season, or, in fact, frequenting balls much at any time (and only now taking interest in her as a near neighbour), he had never heard Harry Egerton's name mentioned in connection with hers.

Harry's conversation after this announcement was, perhaps, a shade more pre-occupied than it had been before. He muttered something about not having been going out much for the last few days—had seen the marriage announced in the *Morning Post*—and therefore supposed that it was to come off.

"It was contradicted, though, afterwards," Grey said. And this was the case.

And if Harry had known that on that Derby morning her brother had handed the paper across the table to Blanche, and told her, with a smile, to read the fashionable intelligence, and that, a moment after, her face had flushed crimson, and she had exclaimed, "How dare they put in such a falsehood?—who can have done this, Charlie?"—if he had known also that a letter had been immediately despatched to say that such an announcement was without the slightest foundation,—and that Galston from that day had been treated with marked coldness,—why, if he had known all this, he might have saved himself many a bitter reflection, and need not now have been reproaching himself for the thoughts which, under those circumstances, he would have had no provocation to indulge in. But his Derby losses, and general distraction of mind, had kept him from taking any notice of the papers, and made him shun society, so that he had not seen or heard anything in contradiction of what he had read.

On parting with Grey he did not prosecute his intention of visiting his aunt. Such delicious reaction from brooding jealousy to renewed assurance of unchanging love was not lightly to be curtailed, until its sweets had been deeply and thoroughly enjoyed; and so he walked on into the park, to realise the intense feeling of relief which had broken, like a wave of joy, upon his heart, rushing and surging through every vein.

"They say she wants to marry somebody else." How he dwelt upon that sentence! With what redoubled tenderness he thought of her now! What a monster he had been ever to dream of doubting her, and to behave coldly to her as he had done of late! It was an intoxicating reverie, into which no thought of present difficulties had the bad taste to intrude. And heedless and unconscious which way he tended, he was borne as it were by some inscrutable magnetic influence into the very presence of the subject of his thoughts.

Absorbed in his luxurious trance, he had loitered on across the park, across the bridge, and in under the shade of those melancholy boughs beyond the water. And here, of a sudden, met his eye a sight which he little thought to see in such a place. In a retired corner, under the shade of one of those dark trees whose lower branches half screened her from the view, was a figure. Why did his heart beat so fast?—Ah! there could be no mistake to his eye. It was Blanche herself, seated, with a book in her hand, gazing absently upon the ground, with so deep a melancholy on her face that the eyes of the elderly attendant who sat by her side almost filled with tears of pitying sympathy as she watched and longed to charm away that sad and sorrowful expression. Do you suppose that Harry, in his present state of feeling, hesitated to intrude upon her thoughts? No. He had some power of self-control, but this was not the moment to exercise it; and, in fact, he never thought of exercising it.

Slightly conscious that his appearance there might seem to be not altogether the result of chance, he approached her chair; and Blanche looked up, started, coloured violently, and held out her hand a little timidly, uncertain whether or not it would be coldly taken.

"I didn't expect to see you here!" he said, as he took it and looked into her face with a depth of tenderness which deepened the colour on her cheek still more.

The maid judiciously rose from her chair to make way for Harry (whose cause had many supporters among the female members of the Mottistone establishment), and Blanche answered that she often came there in the mornings, generally with her father or Charlie. "But they were both busy this morning, and so I brought my maid."

Harry had ere now quietly slipped into the seat vacated by "my maid," who had originally been "my nurse," who was, therefore, a very elderly and respectable chaperone, and a very intelligent one withal,—for she had retired several paces to the rear, and seems to have found some knotty point worth investigating upon a distant tree.

There was a slight pause after Blanche had explained how it was she came to be there; and then Harry said that it was a charming morning.

Charming, wasn't it?

The shade of the old trees was so pleasant.

Delightful! It reminded one of the country.

So cool!

So cool!

Harry had wandered across the park here quite by chance. Didn't know that he was coming there until he found that he was there.

"You must have been thinking very deeply?"

"I was," he answers, absent even now.

With great discernment, the duenna continues her study of nature some little way off; and Harry, after rather an embarrassing pause, continues, looking Blanche full in the face this time—"So you are not going to be married, after all?"

"Did you think I was?" she answered, in such a quiet, reproachful tone, looking on the ground.

"It was only an hour ago I heard that it wasn't true."

A pause—but a very short one. No use trying any longer; it must come out. And his chair seems very much closer to hers now as he exclaims, with passionate eagerness, "I can't bear this suspense any longer Blanche! tell me, only say, that you'll never marry any one but—but me."

He was looking at her with such a wild, eager expression, that Blanche felt almost frightened at his vehemence, as she held out her hand, and, looking very pale now, answered so softly, but with such concentrated meaning, "Never!"

Oh! the rapture of that moment, when that soft little paw was retained within his own, and he looked deep down into the depths of those eyes which were looking into his own with such overflowing love.

"My darling Blanche!" he said, "at last I'm happy!" And so the duenna, who was watching the scene from behind, seemed to think. "You don't know what I've gone through since I heard you were going to marry Galston. But now——" The sentence was not finished. She read the remainder in his look, and he the answer in hers.

That little hand was not released. The minutes flew by apace. The birds sang joyfully overhead, as they looked down from above, and were reminded of the spring. The summer air floated lightly around, and the sunlight chequered the green glades, which were now deserted by nursery-maids and noisy children. No wonder they took no note of time; and no wonder the duenna began to find that even botanical studies are no substitute for dinner.

All earthly delight, however, must some time have an end, and even fainting stomachs be refreshed by hope. But somebody was very late for luncheon, and very incoherent in the excuses which she gave. And though, of course, it all came out afterwards, no one knows so much about the particulars as we do, and I don't think anybody is ever likely to know more.

CHAPTER XV.

Philip Egerton had returned to town a couple of days before. And while Harry's love thoughts were decoying him into the snare which love had laid for him, Philip was creeping home to luncheon in Eaton Place.

As he neared his father's door, a beggar woman, who had been watching the house comes rapidly across the street, sidles up to him, and asks, in a wheedling tone, for money.

Philip walks on without taking any notice, and then she addresses him by name. He turns and looks at her curiously, suspiciously —how did she know his name? But by this time he has reached the door-step, and having nothing to gain, as he thought, by questioning her—probably she was some clever impostor—he proceeds to ascend the steps, threatening to give her in charge of the police if she didn't go away (just as if a policeman was ever to be found in Belgravia, or, for that matter, anywhere that he is wanted). The woman, however, was importunate, said it would be worth his while to listen to her, followed him up the steps, and tried to detain him by taking hold of his arm.

This was too much for Philip's patience. He shook her off angrily, pushing her violently from him, and causing her to stumble and fall upon the steps. Then let himself in with his latch-key, and slammed the door behind him, without looking back, or taking any notice of what had happened.

The woman lay for some minutes, stunned by the fall; and then a passer-by, attracted by her moans, and finding her unable to rise, hailed a cab, and had her conveyed to St. George's Hospital, where, from some internal injury, she was unable at present to give any account of the cause of her accident.

It was not above a minute after she had been removed, when Philip Egerton again opened the door, and looked out. Something had told him that he had acted too hastily in not listening to what she had to say. She knew his name; and now that he thought of it, there was a peculiar meaning expression in her face as she addressed him by that name. What might he, or might he not, have missed, he thought now, as he looked up and down the street, and saw no sign of the woman. There was nothing but a cab in sight, and Philip could not be expected to guess that that cab contained the object of his interest, so he returned again indoors, and endeavoured to dismiss the incident from his thoughts.

Mrs. Greville and Philip lunched alone to-day. The footman believed that Mr. Egerton was in his room. His hat and coat were hanging up in the hall, and his stick was in its usual place.

His sister did not send the servant to inform him that luncheon was ready, for he would have resented it, she thought, as an insult to his punctuality, on which he had been wont to pride himself.

Had been. How little Philip thought what sight would meet his eye when, finding that his father did not come into the dining-room, and having to speak to him on business, he opened his study door some half an hour afterwards, after vainly knocking several times to attract his notice. Mr. Egerton was there, indeed. But it was his lifeless body that met Philip's horrified gaze on entering the room. He was lying back in his chair, his head sunk upon his chest, and a bluish pallor, not to be mistaken, on his face. His hand grasped convulsively the letter which he had been writing when Harry entered, and his fingers had stiffened round it, and were bloodless, cold, and dead.

Philip's knees trembled under him, and his eyes dilated with a shuddering sense of fear and horror at the sight, as he staggered back for a moment against the book-case, and a cold perspiration broke out all over him. Not daring to pass the body to ring the bell, he backed out of the room again in a half-fainting state, and startled the butler in the dining-room by the ashy paleness of his cheek, as he pointed to the study, and gasped out, "Mr. Egerton—is—*dead!*"

What a change there soon came over that usually quiet house! What a hurrying to and fro of footsteps! What scared faces and frightened whispers fill the passages as the doctor hurries past into the room!

Clearly disease of the heart. He had always told Mr. Egerton to be careful of exciting himself. Very sad—fearfully sudden—no cause apparently. What had he been doing that morning?

He had not been out, his servant said. Mr. Henry had been there a little before twelve o'clock, and Mr. Egerton was at that time in his usual health. Since then he had not been seen by any member of the household.

"Mr. Henry was here, did you say?" asked Philip, who had now somewhat recovered his composure.

The footman had shown him into the

study direct, had heard the door shut shortly afterwards, and supposed that he had then gone away.

"Then I fear it is easily to be accounted for, doctor," said Philip, with a well-feigned expression of horror and grief. "You know," he said, "the anxiety my unhappy brother has caused my poor father for the last year or more. An interview with him would naturally excite my father's anger and indignation; and this is the result."

"Henry! Henry! what *have* you done?" cried Mrs. Greville, in the midst of her tears.

"He has killed his father, that is all," replied Philip, assuming a mournful expression, suitable to the occasion, but feeling in his heart a certain vindictive joy, which even the presence of his father's dead body in the adjoining room was unable to repress.

"Don't, don't say that, Philip!" exclaimed his aunt. "Oh, it's too—too horrible!" and she covered her face with her handkerchief, and burst into another paroxysm of weeping.

A messenger shortly after was despatched in search of Harry, and found him at his club.

It was a rude interruption to the delicious thoughts in which he was wrapped (all consideration of the folly of his late proceeding being for the time excluded) to be told that his father was lying dead in his chair, and had not been known to speak since he left the room.

Variously though his emotions had been already tried this day, none, perhaps, had equalled in intensity the pang of horror and remorse which this intelligence occasioned him.

"Good God!" he exclaimed, "what have I done? Am I a murderer?" and the wild look of terror which his face wore as he entered the drawing-room, and threw himself down into a chair, startled Mrs. Greville into comparative composure. He took upon himself all the responsibility and guilt, reproaching himself in the bitterest terms of remorseful anguish as he clasped his hands over his face, and gave way to an agony of uncontrollable grief.

Philip's sarcasms fell pointless upon his ear. The sight of his dead father, from whom he had parted in such bitterness but a few hours before, filled his whole being with such a stunning and absorbing grief, that Mrs. Greville even forgot her own sorrow as she came and knelt beside him, and with gentle sympathy endeavoured to soothe his distracted mind.

What resolutions he made that night as he tossed upon a fevered bed! what vows were registered for a different course of life in future! How earnestly he determined to read aright the lesson he had received, and to turn over a new page, and try, at least, to find some better employment than one which had brought his father to an untimely grave! By what fearful dreams were the harrowing recollections of the day succeeded! and what a terrible awakening there came on the morning following that night!

CHAPTER XVI.

Private grief is not respected by duns. It may be that sometimes they don't know what they are intruding upon. But men say they want their money, and that is to them a sufficient excuse for disregarding any sentimental considerations.

Harry Egerton found it so. Letter after letter was brought to him in the midst of his engrossing sorrow, applying for payment, and threatening further measures. And, in spite of himself, he couldn't help thinking that now there was a chance of his being able to pay, since his father's death would put him into possession of his mother's fortune.

Explanation to that effect was given to the most pressing of his creditors; and he even told Mr. Villars that he hoped now (and he alluded with a sort of awe to the subject) to be in a position to enter some profession, which should lessen the folly and imprudence he had been guilty of in proposing to marry his daughter *in formâ pauperis*. It was a comfort, indeed, to have such sympathy as Blanche's in his present grief, and to be able to think of their marriage being not so far distant now as some days before it had appeared.

But all this subdued delight of anticipation, which counteracted, to a certain extent, the shadow which past events had cast upon his thoughts, was rudely dispelled one morning by a letter from his brother in the following terms:—

" My dear Henry," it began, " in consequence of my dear father's lamented death —allusion to which must be so painful to *you*—I have, as you know, for the last few days been engaged in the arrangement of his papers.

" You are aware, I believe, that my father made no will previous to his death, and that being the case, you will see, of course, that you have no claim upon any portion of his property. Now, although I have ever thought that my poor father showed too great kindness—I might almost say weakness—in continuing to give you a fixed allowance in the face of your undutiful behaviour and extravagant habits, I have, notwithstanding, determined to continue to you the annual sum which you were in receipt of during the last year of my father's life;— this, too, although the expenses of succession duty, and other matters, would naturally require that I should have as few additional charges as possible just at present.

"But, while I consider that such a concession is due to what might have been my poor father's wishes had he lived to express them, I must impress upon you that, without some alteration becomes apparent in your present style of living, I shall not hold myself justified in sacrificing my own interests for the support of your vicious follies. The calamity which you have been instrumental in bringing upon the family should teach you a lesson, at least, and make you thankful that *one* of my father's sons has sufficient sense of duty to carry out what he believed to be his parent's wishes, even though they may not have been expressed in words.

"I remain,
"Very faithfully yours,
"Philip Egerton."

The angry flush of indignation grew deeper and deeper upon Harry's face as he read, and when he came to the end, he threw the letter from him with an expression of unmitigated disgust.

"Well, if that isn't the dirtiest piece of composition I ever read," he exclaimed, "I don't know what is! He makes a favour of continuing that miserable two hundred a year. No mention of my mother's money at all. But I'm hanged if I stand this," he added, and then and there seized his hat and issued forth in the direction of Eaton Place.

Philip was at home, and Harry was straightway ushered into his presence.

"Good morning, Philip," he said, shortly and firmly.

"Good morning," rejoined Philip, looking up inquiringly from a parchment upon which he was engaged. "I wrote to you last night," he said. "Did you not receive my letter?"

"Yes, I did receive it," Harry answered, "and it's about that letter that I have come here."

Philip folded his hands, and resting his arms on either side of his chair, said—"I am not aware that it contains any matter for discussion. The terms of it, I think, were sufficiently plain."

"Perfectly plain," rejoined Harry, sitting down on the other side of the table, with the letter in his hand. "But you make no mention of that twenty thousand pounds of my mother's which was to come to me at my father's death."

"There certainly was a sum of that kind received by my father upon his marriage; but I find no mention of its settlement upon you amongst his papers."

"Well, that shows you, at any rate, that he intended that it should be so settled, even if you didn't know it before." And Harry handed over for Philip's inspection his father's letter to that intent, which Greville had furnished him with not long before.

Philip read it through without moving a muscle of his face, and then answered— "This appears to be merely a private note of my poor father's, which is interesting, of course, from its antiquity. But in a legal point of view I fear you will find it only a morsel of waste paper."

"I know that it isn't of any use in point of law; but it shows you, what you knew before, that it was always my father's intention that the money should revert to me. My aunt can tell you the same if you like to ask her."

"Really, it is impossible for me to conjecture——"

"Conjecture!" exclaimed Harry. "Why, there it is before you in black and white."

"To conjecture," Philip continued, without noticing the interruption, "what intentions my father might have had, when I find none expressed in any legal form amongst his papers. It would hardly be right for me to make over to you so large a sum of money on the warrant of a piece of paper such as this. Was that the only point upon which you wished to speak to me? I'm afraid I shall scarcely be able to fall in with your views upon the subject."

The cool and deliberate way in which he spoke roused Harry's indignation quite up to boiling point, and he exclaimed, with angry vehemence—

"Do you mean to say, then, that you refuse to take any notice of my father's known wishes, and that you intend to appropriate that money to yourself?"

"If you call taking legal possession of one's natural property appropriation, you may, I suppose, apply the term in the present instance. For I see no cause as yet to prevent my entering into full possession, as eldest son, of all my father's property."

"And yet you congratulate yourself that *one* member of the family (reading Philip's letter) has a sufficient sense of duty to carry out what he believed to be his father's wishes, even though they may not have been expressed in words. And notwithstanding that they have been expressed, both in words and in writing, you don't consider it *right* to carry them out. What a delicious consistency!"

Harry's anger so far carried him away that he forgot his prudence altogether—forgot that it was entirely in Philip's power to withhold even the wretched sum which he now proposed to pay. And he treated him to such a frank expression of his opinion upon his conduct, that Philip, who had contemplated him all the time with a cold eye and lurking smile, replied at last—that when he so far forgot his nature as to encourage his brother in his reckless dissipation by continuing his allowance, he had hardly expected that his gratitude would take so demonstrative a form. It might now be necessary for him to reconsider his decision, since he found that it met with so little appreciation.

About that Harry said that he might do as he pleased. But that he didn't intend to be done out of money which was properly his, and so Philip would see.

Philip smiled at the impotent threat, and rejoined cuttingly—

"Are you quite sure that even if the money had been settled upon the younger children of the marriage, you could prove your claim to it? For I am not at all so confident upon that point."

"What do you mean?" cried Harry.

"I mean only what I say. But it is not necessary for me to detain you any longer. Your time, no doubt, is valuable."

With that Philip stretched out his hand to the bell-rope, and rang the bell. And Harry, stifling his wrath as well as he was able, and a little confused at the probability of Philip's casual suggestion, declared that he would have an explanation and see that justice was done, and slamming the door violently after him, left the house.

Philip continued to smile after he left the room, was glad that the explanation which he knew must come had been got through, and congratulated himself on having evidently put a spoke in his brother's wheel by suggesting that doubt about his title. He must work it all out when he had time. Why hadn't he listened to that woman at the door? She haunted him, he couldn't tell why; she must have had something to say about this very subject. If he only knew for certain, what a triumph it would be! Harry might whistle for an allowance then. And with such thoughts floating about his mind Philip again bent his attention upon the parchment before him.

CHAPTER XVII.

From Philip's presence his brother betook himself straight to Lincoln's Inn, and was once more in the sanctum of Mr. Naylor Bond, who from some unnatural impulse of vanity had mounted a small red tie to-day, so that he looked more than ever now like one of his own parchments tied up with a piece of red tape. There was very little satisfaction, however, to be got from Mr. Naylor Bond. The money, he said, was not settled; and, therefore, it was quite impossible for Harry to prove a right to it. He had suggested to Mr. Philip Egerton that it had been his father's intention to have some such deed made, but that he had never received instructions to draw one out; and Mr. Philip Egerton had said that that was a pity, for then he should have been able to act in the matter. And the lawyer smiled grimly as he recorded the brother's answer.

So then one more hope is knocked on the head, poor Harry thought as he walked listlessly away from the abode of law; and his feelings towards his brother at this moment were of a most unfraternal nature indeed. Then he remembered that Philip had taunted him with the possibility of there being a flaw even in his title to the name he bore; and his aunt's still unexplained letter now came back with full force upon his mind. His interest in Lady Belvedere's romance had given way for a time to the poignancy of the remorse and grief which his father's death had occasioned him; and no further light having as yet been thrown upon it, matters of more immediate interest had lately occupied his thoughts. Even Lady Belvedere herself was growing a little used to the suspense and nervous agitation which had prevented her feeling as annoyed as she otherwise would have been at her brother's death.

For gaiety, and breakfasts, and weddings had perforce given way to her nerves, and she would in any case have been obliged to keep to the house for some days past.

But as day succeeded day without any confirmation of that singular letter being sent, her interest in the gossip and news of the town with which female friends kept her *au courant* revived, and Harry had a few days before undergone a severe lecture upon the folly of engaging himself to a girl comparatively without money, when there was an heiress of Lady Belvedere's providing only waiting to be asked to marry him at once.

This morning, however, her ladyship had again been thrown into a state of nerves by a visit from an Italian priest—the writer, as he informed her, of that preparative letter which had been the subject of her thoughts for so many days.

Would Harry believe it, she asked hysterically, when he came to see her that afternoon—her son whom she had so long supposed to be in his grave, was actually a priest in a Jesuit college abroad! There could be no doubt of the truth of what the man had alleged, he had given her such convincing proof on every point. Circumstances had hitherto delayed him from coming forward to assert his rights; but now he was going to claim his estates, and part of her property, too, for the benefit of his order.

Lady Belvedere, however strongly inclined towards Rome, was not prepared to find a son in a ready-made priest, who, moreover, would despoil her of a considerable portion of the handsome income which, in default of a son, she had hitherto enjoyed; and her disappointment and irritation were not, therefore, to be wondered at under the circumstances. But Harry, it must be confessed, had not so much sympathy to offer now that it had all been cleared up in this unexpected way. He listened almost in silence to his aunt's account of her interview with the priest; and when he went away, he felt more disconsolate and spirit-broken than ever—one light after another had gone out, and all again was complete darkness.

What could Philip mean? he wondered

more than ever now; and then he thought with a pang of the disappointment which Blanche must necessarily feel, when he told her that he had gone back to where he was when in his folly he had made her promise to marry him—a poor devil without a sixpence, and with debts enough to swamp a moderate fortune. At this moment, as he neared the club, his eyes fell upon the ragged form of his broken-down cousin loitering about before the door; and in his present mood the sight was an irritating one.

Harassed though he had been of late with every kind of anxiety and care, he had not forgotten his promise to him; and had yesterday sent some small sum to keep him going until he himself had more funds at his command to assist him with. But however benevolently disposed he might be towards the man, it was not altogether agreeable to find him hanging about St. James's Street, presumably with the object of meeting with his benefactor; for in his present state of dress and appearance he was not exactly the companion that a smart young man would have chosen to walk arm-in-arm with down that street.

I daresay some such thought as this found expression in Harry's face, for his cousin explained that he should not have presumed to seek him out in this locality if he had not had important matter to communicate. He had tried to find out Harry's address at his father's house, but had been turned away from the door without an answer; and he had not written, because he thought that he might not get the letter from there. So he had waited, hoping every day to hear from him, and on receipt of his letter that morning had lost no time in coming to look for him at the address therein contained.

Harry listened, a little impatiently perhaps, to this explanation, and carelessly wondering what he could have to tell, desired him to come with him to his lodgings.

Having briefly explained the meaning of his deep mourning, he hurried on at once to the object of his cousin's appearance; and his languid interest was soon arrested, as the latter gradually unburdened himself of his tale. The first emotion of surprise gave way to a strained eagerness, which became absolutely painful as the other proceeded; and his parted lips and riveted attention showed plainly enough that it was matter of no ordinary concern to him which was being narrated.

"And you know where this woman is?" he exclaimed at last, excitedly.

Unfortunately he did not. He had not seen her since that day.

Harry was silent for a moment.

"You don't know her name—where she could be found?—is there no way of finding her?"

Not unless she was known to the police, perhaps. But without knowing her name it wouldn't be easy to set any inquiry on foot.

Harry was silent again for a moment or two—then starting up he seized a pen, and dashed off a letter to Mr. Naylor Bond (to let off his excitement, it seemed, more than for any practical purpose), saying that he had just received most unexpected intelligence, which would prove that his brother had no claim to his father's estate—in fact that he was either illegitimate or somebody else's son—he was not yet in possession of all the particulars—would write again, or come and see him.

Having thus relieved the high pressure of his feelings by imparting to another the news which had occasioned them to be wrought up to their present tension, he put on his hat again, descended the stairs two steps at a time, barely waited to tell his cousin to engage a lodging for himself in the neighbourhood and let him know where to find him, jumped into a Hansom, and was off to see Mrs. Greville, in Curzon Street, whither she had removed from Philip's establishment.

Mrs. Greville had just gone out. Lady Farringford was also out. How very provoking! What was he to do to pass the time till she returned? He would wait in the drawing-room—particularly wanted to see Mrs. Greville. So he deposited himself on a sofa—sat there for a few minutes in a state of nervous impatience—got up and went to the table—took up one book after another, and threw them down again—went and looked out of the window—then rang the bell, and asked for the second time how long it was since the carriage had left the door—tried to sit down again after the servant left the room, but sprang up a moment after and left the house, saying that he would return again in an hour or so—called a cab, and directed the driver to Lincoln's Inn—had got about half-way, when he stopped him again, having decided that until he had seen Mrs. Greville it would be of no use to go down there again—paid the cabman, and walked back again to Curzon Street, and found the carriage at the door.

Mrs. Greville and Maud were in the drawing-room, and looked at him in surprise, as he came into the room with an unusually quick step and flurried air.

"At last, I've found out your secret,

aunt!" he cried, without further greeting. "Why couldn't you have told me this before? Philip, I find, is not my father's son."

Mrs. Greville started, looked at him with amazement for a moment, and then sank down upon the sofa. The suddenness of the announcement had been rather much for her weak nerves. "My *dear* Henry," she gasped, "who told you this?"

"Frank; he had it from his own mother. My eldest brother died when he was a few days old."

Mrs. Greville still looked at him, as if unable to realise the intelligence; and it was some moments before she recovered her composure sufficiently to assert that she had always said that it must come out.

Harry now pressed for an immediate disclosure of all she knew upon the subject; and, as he had found out so much for himself, and as her brother's wrath had not now the terrors for her which formerly had restrained her from divulging her suspicions, there was no longer any occasion to withhold what little knowledge she possessed. Practically, it was not much, and when she came to the end of it, Harry was a little disappointed. Its purport was as follows:—Mrs. Egerton, as we know, had been confined at Castle Greville; her life for some time had been despaired of, and it was not for many days, therefore, after its birth that she had seen her child. Mrs. Greville, however, was in the habit of paying periodical visits to the nursery, and on one of these occasions had noticed such an unaccountable change in the baby's appearance that she had remarked upon it to the nurse, and had been considerably struck by the oddness and confusion of her replies. Full of anxiety at the time about Mrs. Egerton herself, she had allowed the matter partly to escape her attention, and had hardly recurred to it again until after the mother's recovery. She then heard that the steward's wife,—a woman for whom she had always had a particular aversion, and whose character in the place was of the very worst, —had been confined about the same time as Mrs. Egerton, and that her child had died a few days after its birth. This woman was now frequently to be seen in the nursery, or accompanying the nurse in her walks; and Mrs. Greville was informed by her maid that it was believed among the servants that she had some secret power over the nurse, resulting (as by occasional hints Mrs. M'Pherson had made it appear) from some former slip which it was whispered that she herself had aided and abetted. Much more tattle to the same effect Mrs. Greville listened to ; and after further comparing of dates, and questioning of the nurse, she became so fully convinced in her own mind that a fraud had been perpetrated, if not a deliberate murder committed, that she had at last communicated her suspicions to her brother. But he had flown into such a passion at the mere suggestion, supposed that she had been telling that to his wife, to help her recovery, and treated her whole story with such angry contempt, that she had only once again dared to mention the subject afterwards; and then he had become so violent at the supposition that he was bringing up a changeling, and had so peremptorily desired that the matter might never be mentioned again, that she had ever since carefully avoided any approach to family matters. And although she had never been able to look upon Philip as her brother's son, in deference to his wishes she had refrained from doing more than occasionally hint at a mystery, fully persuaded, as she again said, that it must all come out some day. And what a relief it was to her to think that it had, and so opportunely too!

"You may be sure, Henry," she said, "that I would not have willingly kept anything from you that it was to your advantage to know; but your poor dear father——" Mrs. Greville here raised her handkerchief to her eyes again,—"and, after all," she continued, "I had no proof at all that I was right, such as you have now."

Maud had listened in astonishment and delight to her mother's recital, and now congratulated Harry with the most extravagant joy, taking it for granted that he would at once enter into possession.

"This woman, who calls herself his mother, will have to be found first, my dear Maud," said Harry. "M'Pherson, did you say her name was, aunt?"

"That was the steward's name. I have never forgotten it."

"It must be the same, I should think."

"Sure to be," Maud said. "And I can't tell you how glad I am, Harry," she added. "I never could bear Philip. And it's so delightful to know that I may hate him now as much as I like."

Harry, however, knew very well that a good deal more proof would be required before Maud could legitimately indulge her freedom of thought. At present his case rested upon Mrs. Greville's suppositions and Frank Egerton's unsupported assertion. The question was how to find the woman herself. It was something, however, to have got at her name, for of course these two were one and the same person.

In his restless eagerness to push on the

matter at once, it was irritating to think that at present he didn't know how to proceed. He was almost sorry he had despatched that letter in such precipitate haste to Lincoln's Inn. It was too late to go down there now. His anxiety and suspense would have to be endured till the following day. But as he had had a good deal of practice lately in bearing suspense, and becoming calm under exciting circumstances, he managed to pass the evening without utterly prostrating his nervous system.

If Harry had continued his way to Mr. Naylor Bond's office that afternoon, he would have had the good fortune to meet his brother in the room at that very time.

Philip Egerton having got over that disagreeable interview with Harry in the morning, had said to himself, "Soul take thine ease, for thou hast goods laid up in store for many years"—had rang for his servant shortly after, and informed him that he was going down into Leicestershire that evening for two or three days.

During the course of the afternoon, on his way to the station, he had called to see his solicitor on one or two little matters of business, and had found him fresh from the perusal of Harry's incoherent note.

"Have you heard anything of this, Mr. Egerton?" said he, handing over the open letter which he held in his hand.

Philip read it through.

"So he thinks I'm not my father's son, does he? 'either illegitimate, or somebody else's.' I wonder who his informant may be," Philip continued, chuckling at the notion of Harry having discovered a mare's nest, which he (Philip) knew so much more about than Harry could. He had evidently got hold of the wrong end of the stick. So delightfully confident too. It was delicious.

The lawyer looked with a most puzzled air at the singular reception which such an announcement as that contained in the letter was meeting with from the party chiefly concerned.

"You know something of it, then?" he said.

"Something; perhaps a little more than your correspondent," Philip answered, smiling pleasantly. And he proceeded to enlighten the lawyer upon his acquaintance and interviews with Mr. Flint and his successor.

"But you are sure you could not be mistaken?—that you could not have misunderstood him?" asked the wary lawyer.

"Quite," Philip replied, with an easy confidence. "If that old man could only be made to give up whatever this information is which he holds, we might settle Master Henry's hash in a very short space of time."

The lawyer, perhaps, would just as soon have had Mr. Philip's hash settled; but he replied—

"Is he so very close? He might, surely, be tempted with a good offer of money?"

"He was not open to terms when last I saw him." But here a happy thought occurred to Philip, and he continued: "What if you were to write to him, and explain that, having reason to believe that the information which he possesses will confute a claim which the person who calls himself Mr. Henry Egerton is proposing to advance against the late Mr. Egerton's eldest son, your client will be prepared to consider whatever terms he may require for the furnishing of that information? Of course, if it was not worth having, I should not entertain his proposals. He must give some idea of its nature before he is paid for it. I don't know this man's name,—never could find it out; but address the letter to Flint, and he will be sure to open it."

Not altogether unwillingly, Mr. Naylor Bond obeyed his client's instructions. It was not that he wanted to persecute Harry, but rather that he thought it was possible that Philip Egerton might have been misled by old Flint, and that Harry's case might receive additional strength from the testimony Philip was so eager to obtain. He knew better than his client what pettifogging lawyers were.

He said nothing further, however, on the subject to Philip; and the letter having been written and despatched, Philip transacted his business, and went on into the country in high good-humour at the prospect of making Harry look so very foolish at some, he hoped, not distant day. It did puzzle him, however, to divine where he could possibly have got the suggestion upon which he had jumped to such a false conclusion. His aunt was the only person he could think of likely to know;—wasn't it like a woman to make a confusion of the kind? And Philip drove up to his own door, through his own trees, with a conscious pride of possession which was very pleasant to enjoy, and which soon ousted Harry and his machinations from his mind.

CHAPTER XVIII.

Next morning Harry was again in the family solicitor's room.

"This is a sudden change which has taken place in your prospects, Mr. Henry," he said, as they shook hands. "Have you good reason to suppose that there is any foundation for the statements which you make in your note of yesterday?"

"Excellent reasons!" Harry replied, cheerfully; and he was proceeding to give Mr. Bond the details of his cousin's intelligence, and Mrs. Greville's corroboration, when the other interrupted him—

"Excuse me one moment; that letter came for you this morning under cover to me."

He took the letter, glanced at the address, and went on with his narrative, the lawyer listening attentively to every point, and nodding his head at each successive pause.

"Your case at present, then," he said, when Harry had finished, "as I apprehend it, stands thus: A certain woman, who is not forthcoming, has declared, very recently, that the late Mr. Egerton's presumed eldest son is no son of his at all; that he is her son, and that he was exchanged in some way, not yet accounted for, in early infancy,— Mrs. Egerton's child having previously or subsequently died, — which statement, at present, is only supported by the individual conviction of Mrs. Greville. Not a very strong case, my dear sir, I must confess."

"Not as yet," Harry admitted; "but if this woman, M'Pherson, can be found, and turns out to be identical with the one who originated my cousin's story?"

"Stronger, but not strong enough to turn out a man in possession. "Is the nurse still living?"

"Yes," Harry answered, eagerly, "she is. And if she were to swear to the truth of what the other said,—that, and my aunt's evidence, and, I dare say, more that might be collected, wouldn't that be strong enough?"

The lawyer smiled at his eagerness. "You may find it difficult to hit upon this woman, M'Pherson, unless, indeed, she turns up of her own accord, which, if she is the one whom your cousin mentions, is likely enough. But doesn't it strike you as improbable that she would not have made use of her knowledge before now, if what she says is true?"

Harry was obliged to confess that it would have been strange. "But there may have been some good reason to prevent her that we don't know of."

After a slight pause, the lawyer continued: "I don't know that I am violating your brother's confidence in telling you that he has reason to suppose that you are under a mistake—(he was here yesterday afternoon, and I showed him your letter)—that, from information which he has from another source, he has for some time past been under the impression that there was a doubt about your own claim to be recognised as Mr. Egerton's son,—but would you mind opening the letter you have there? It occurs to me now that the contents may bear upon the subject we are discussing."

Harry complied with the request, and unfolded a half-sheet of foolscap paper. "Rose M'Pherson!" he exclaimed, as the name caught his eye at once on opening the document. And as he glanced rapidly down the contents, the lawyer smiled again at the joyful elation upon his features.

"Well, this is the oddest bit of luck!" he exclaimed at last, as he finished reading, and handed over the paper to Bond, his eyes sparkling with the unexpected light which apparently had been thrown upon his case.

The paper in question was the copy of an affidavit made by this very woman whom he was anxious to find, duly attested by a commissioner, and the court in which the original was filed also specified.

"With this, or the original of this, at your command," said the lawyer, "you scarcely require to find the woman. But I should be curious to know under what circumstances it was made."

"Ah!" he continued, reading a small note at the foot of the page, "'Copied by T. Flint, October 20th, 18—.' This, then, is his answer to my note of yesterday." And he told Harry the nature of the letter which he had written at Philip's suggestion.

Now, wasn't that a strange old man? It was not filthy lucre, after all, that he had been aiming at in refusing to give up the information he possessed. Obstinacy, suspicion, and dislike, followed up now by revenge for Philip's threats on the occasion of their last interview, seem to have been the feelings which influenced him; and sending such an answer to Philip's letter must have been a triumph indeed.

Mr. Bond, shrewdly enough, guessed that this affidavit had been made at the instigation of old Flint, and that he had proposed to make a nice little profit to himself out of it, had he not been so suddenly removed from the scene of his labours.

The circumstances under which the exchange of children had taken place were sworn to in effect as follows:—

Mrs. M'Pherson had already entertained the design of making use of her influence over the nurse for the purpose of a fraud of the kind, and had sounded her victim more than once upon the subject, without actually expressing her meaning. Matters had as yet gone no further, when the nurse burst into her room one morning early (her husband being away at the time), and informed her, with a terrified face, that Mrs. Egerton's child was dead—lain upon in the night—killed, in fact, by her. What was she to do? They would try her for murder. Couldn't the other help her? Here was the opportunity ready made for the Scotchwoman; and she worked upon the other's fears so effectually, that the exchange was made without further delay, Mrs. Egerton's child buried and mourned over as hers, and her sad bereavement duly imparted to her husband on his return.

"If you can find out the nurse, and get her to corroborate all this," said the lawyer, "your case will not be quite so bad as it seemed at first. But I'm puzzled to think why this claim has not been advanced before, and how she got into Flint's hands."

Harry could offer no solution, except by finding the woman herself. How could that be done?

Mr. Bond promised to think it over. "But in the meantime," he said, "you should secure the evidence of the nurse, if, as you say, you know where to find her."

Harry said that he should write to Greville immediately—that afternoon.

"I shall of course be obliged to communicate with your—I suppose I must still call him brother—with reference to the danger in which he stands of losing his property. In fact, as I am properly acting for him, I am not sure that I ought to have given you advice in the matter."

Harry begged that he would not apologise; told him that he was perfectly at liberty to lay all the particulars before Philip; hoped that he would not be disappointed at the result of his investigations; promised that

Mr. Bond should hear of him again shortly, and took his leave, with the copy of Mrs. M'Pherson's affidavit in his pocket, and lightness indescribable in his heart.

Mr. Naylor Bond pondered for a few moments over the mutability of human affairs, and reflected philosophically upon the strange coincidence of evidence which in one day had accumulated to invalidate a title which there had not seemed the slightest doubt about before; and then settled himself to communicate to his client, as pleasantly as might be, the unexpected result of his letter to the attorney, and the undoubtedly strong case which Harry would have against him, if he obtained corroborative evidence from the nurse herself.

As Philip had not mentioned that he was going into the country, the letter was sent to Eaton Place, and did not come into his hands until his return two or three days after.

Harry, meanwhile, had written to Greville, and, on second thoughts, had decided to follow up his letter in person. He was, therefore, already in Ireland before Philip became aware of the mine which was being sprung under his feet.

When he did return, however, and read that letter from his lawyer—what a sight was Philip then to see! Livid with disappointed hate, which had so unexpectedly recoiled upon himself,—maddened by the thought that all the while he had fancied he was advancing his own interest and promoting Harry's ruin, he had only been making his own ultimate dispossession the more easy—furious at the prospect of being deprived of what he had only just with such anticipation entered upon the enjoyment of—cursing his folly in not having propitiated that old man—fool, too, that he had been not to take notice of that woman who had endeavoured to detain him at his door, could it be that that creature was his mother? Stung with an agony of envy at the thought of Harry succeeding to the wealth which he should have to relinquish, and having it in his power to repay the treatment which he had received at his hands

—but no; he never should! Philip determined that nothing should make him give up his newly-acquired lands and money—he wouldn't let them go without a struggle. Harry had not yet proved his title, and he might find it harder than he thought. But Philip, as he cast about for a way to escape what promised to be the conclusive nature of the evidence to be brought against him, could find no loop-hole—his solicitor could only suggest that possession was nine points of the law. Strong proof would be required on the side of the petitioner. But yet, if the nurse's evidence was trustworthy, Mr. Philip Egerton's tenure hardly promised to be of long duration.

How Philip hated them all round, and how he writhed in impotent rage and mortification as he looked upon his position and saw no way of escape from it! But stop!—that nurse—could she not be——? And Philip left for Ireland by that night's mail.

CHAPTER XIX.

Most people, I suppose, during the course of a long or short existence, have at one time or another indulged in day-dreams of imaginary wealth, and discounted the delicious feelings they would experience if it were suddenly announced to them that they had come in for a property. Life has been all at once invested with new charms. Numberless hitherto impossible pleasures will now be at their command. The minutest details of what they will do with their sudden acquisition of means have been dwelt upon with all the relish of anticipation. They have settled in their own minds who shall come and stay with them, what good offices they will now be enabled to perform for their friends, what kindnesses it will now be in their power to requite, what former incivility a proportionate coldness will now repay. They have pictured themselves surrounded by their guests in their own house. They have played the host with inimitable courtesy and grace. And they have observed with gratification the increased respect which their altered position inspires.

Most people, then, will be able to understand the feelings which passed away the time so rapidly to Harry Egerton, as he lay coiled up in the corner of the carriage, on his way to Ireland. The sudden turn which his affairs had taken had almost bewildered him at first; and it was not until a day or two after that he began to get accustomed to the thought that now there really did seem a prospect of a break in the clouds. The excitement and agitation of the previous days had calmed down a little now. And he was in the full enjoyment of undisputed possession. Not alone either—Elysian thought! It was still too good almost to be a prospective reality. He never could expect to enjoy such unalloyed happiness as his imagination represented for him, if his journey were successful. Would he live to enjoy it? he thought; and then conjured up all sorts of improbable contingencies to spoil his dream of expectation.

In due course, however, he arrived in Dublin, met Greville there, and went down with him at once into Galway, Greville being only too glad to afford him every facility for clearing up the mystery which the year before he had so incredulously ridiculed. If it had been Philip who required his assistance, it is possible that it might not have been given quite so readily.

Bringing with them a commissioner, that the woman's evidence might be taken down in a legal form, they proceeded to her cabin.

She was rocking herself to and fro before the turf fire, with a low moaning sound, as they entered; and she recognised her unexpected visitors with a terrified start, and a wild dramatic gesticulation of fright, as she shrank away into a corner.

Harry began now to entertain serious doubts as to the trustworthiness of such a witness. And Greville, holding out his hand, began talking to her quietly about herself for a time,—gradually, and reluctantly on her part, leading her back to her experience as a nurse in Mr. Egerton's family, and at last asking her whether she remembered Mrs. M'Pherson, the steward's wife, who was there at that time.

The old woman had been regarding him as he spoke with a cunning, uneasy expression, which now found vent in—"Who would she be at all, your honour? It's none of that name that ever *I* had dealings with."

"Not about a child that died?" Greville asked, quietly.

"Died!" she exclaimed, almost with a shriek. "Then it wasn't murder, though she told me it was. Ha! ha! no murder, after all!"

Her face suddenly resumed its fixed and cunning expression, and she said, "What child was that at all, your honour? Wasn't his brother" (pointing at Harry) "the only one ever I nursed?"

Greville here produced the copy of the

affidavit which Harry had brought with him, and read it over to her, looking up every now and then to see how she was affected by it.

At first she looked at him from under her shaggy eyebrows with a suspicious and apprehensive glance; but as he read on, and the recollections of former days and acts were brought vividly before her again, Harry saw the same wild look of terror come into her face; and before Spencer had finished reading, she threw herself on the ground at his feet, and declared that she would tell him all if he only wouldn't be hard upon her in her old age, when she was better than in her grave already.

"Speak for me, Master Henry!" she cried, clinging about his knees. "I wouldn't have wronged you, darlin', for all the gold in Ireland. God Almighty witness that it's the truth I'm telling! but she told me I'd murdered the poor wee thing, and I'd be hanged for murder. And it was herself that put me up to it; and now to go and tell on me! But it's well for her that she'll get nothing by it now!" And, amid a profusion of regrets, imprecations, prayers, and entreaties for mercy, the old woman was prevailed upon at last to tell her story in an intelligible form.

Substantially it bore out the statement of the woman who claimed to be Philip Egerton's real mother. The child had been introduced as there alleged. The nurse had been kept on in the family, against her will, but at Mrs. M'Pherson's command she had consented to remain, and to go abroad with Mr. Egerton afterwards. It was a sorry time she had had of it ever since that deed was done, she said; for although this woman, M'Pherson, had left Castle Greville before they returned from Italy, she had written from time to time, reminding her of what the probable consequences would be if she ever disclosed the fraud. And though it was many years now since she had had word from her, yet the influence of her threats, and the strange power which she had exercised over her, still remained; and the consciousness of having that secret upon her mind, and the penalty of disclosing it, had made her an older woman at five-and-forty than her own mother was at seventy. The neighbours had ascribed her incoherent ravings to the shock which it was presumed the drowning of her husband had caused her; but he could have told them that, long before his death, his sleep had been broken in upon at nights by her strange exclamations and restless regrets, which he was not long in reducing to some more coherent meaning.

So she rambled on, garnishing her tale with many an ejaculation and entreaty to be spared. And when the material points had been taken down and sworn to before the legal functionary in waiting, Greville again reassured her on the score of her personal liberty, provided she would swear to all this in a court of law, if required, and then returned with Harry to the house.

One more link was thus completed in the chain which was to wrest from Philip's grasp the wealth which he would have used so well; and the next day was spent in further strengthening this link by collecting many little items of circumstantial evidence in the neighbourhood. Harry suggested the priest; but was told that he never could divulge what had come to his ears in confession.

"Here you see one of the beauties of that system," Greville said. "He has known all along, I suppose, that this was going on, and was obliged to look on quietly, without taking any steps to see that justice was done."

In further illustration of the advantages of such aids to morality as confession, Greville instanced a case in a neighbouring county, where a friend of his own had been shot at, recognised the would-be murderer, sworn to him, and had him subsequently hanged.

"It came out afterwards," he said, "that there was every reason to suppose that the man who was hanged was not the guilty one. There was another strangely resembling him in the neighbourhood; and it is generally believed there now that he is the man who ought to have been hanged, and not the other. The priest knew that an innocent man was suffering, couldn't break his confessional oath, and, as the doctor who attended him assured me, died not very long after from the effects of having such a load upon his mind."

The priest, therefore, could not be counted upon, but various other not unimportant witnesses were found; and, on the following day, they were again *en route* for Dublin.

A few miles from the point where they would hit upon the railway, they were passed by another car, whereon sat a solitary individual, muffled, and apparently deep in thought, for he had not the curiosity to raise his head as they passed.

From the nature of the Irish car it is possible, though not usual, for the occupants of the left side of the car to pass without seeing each other. Not usual, because in Ireland the right, and not the left, is the side for passing. Possibly it may have been so ordained in consideration of the car being the usual mode of conveyance, and the Irish nature being of that sociable kind which makes it a pleasure for a man to turn his face instead of his back to a casual stranger. Facility would thereby be afforded for those amenities of the road in which it delights that Irish nature to indulge.

However, such facility was not afforded in the present instance, for the two cars, owing to the intervention of perverse cattle, passed each other on the wrong side, and the drivers only had that full view of each other's countenances which is ordinarily conceded to the passengers. It happened, therefore, that the solitary individual, muffled, and apparently in deep thought, did not see the occupants of the other car. But he was inspected by them as they drove asunder; and Greville was startled by a sudden exclamation from Harry: "Why, Spencer, I'd almost take my oath that that was Philip on that car!"

"Not likely, my dear Harry," said Greville, as he looked carelessly after the retreating figure. "That man has whiskers, too. Philip has no whiskers."

That was true, Harry admitted; but still

he thought he couldn't be mistaken in those features; and after all, he said, Philip was quite capable of anything. He was very glad they had that woman's evidence taken down.

It wasn't likely, Greville said, that he would come over when he knew Harry was there.

"But perhaps he doesn't know it. I never told Bond I was coming."

And Philip did not know it, or he might have saved himself the journey. For when, after careful inquiry, he had ferreted out the cabin of his former nurse, all the satisfaction which his threats had extracted from the suspicious fears of the woman had been the disagreeable information that he had been forestalled, and that all she knew of the matter was now in writing, and sworn to by herself as completely as he could desire. Philip threw down the implement with which he had threatened to dash out her brains if she didn't answer his questions, flung a curse at the unfortunate creature whom he had nearly frightened out of whatever wits she still retained, and in an hour's time was on his way back to London, missing the pleasure of travelling in Harry's company by one mail only.

CHAPTER XX.

WHAT a radiant face was Blanche's as she entered the breakfast-room two or three days after Harry's departure for Ireland, holding in her hand a letter just received from him, in which he explained all that he had only hinted at before for fear of raising hopes which might ultimately be disappointed, in which he assured her that now he had no doubt but that within a very short time he should—but his glowing periods were very properly reserved for private re-perusal, and only the parts which bore upon the strange events of the last few days communicated to profane ears.

Breakfast was, of course, suspended to listen to and marvel at such unexpected news, and very sincere indeed were the wishes expressed for Harry's success and a brighter promise for Blanche's love.

News of this kind does not often break in upon a breakfast table, and Blanche, very naturally, was quite above the necessity for food. In fact, there was very little eating done at all this morning, so engrossed were the whole party with the contents of that letter.

Mr. Villars very considerately did not mar the general joy by hinting at the possibility of an interminable lawsuit; and Lady Mary's loving, sympathetic look, as she gazed into Blanche's sparkling eyes, fully expressed all the pleasure she felt in the anticipation of her child's happiness.

Now that it had all come out, Charlie said he could remember more than one expression of Harry's which had puzzled him at the time, but which seemed now to imply that he had always had some suspicion of something being wrong. "And as for that fellow who calls himself his brother," he said, "I don't think anybody will be very sorry for him. I always used to feel quite uncomfortable whenever he was in the room. I never heard anyone, I think, say a good word for him."

How lightly sped the hours of that day, winged with joy, and hope, and love! And what a meeting that was on the following morning, when Blanche comes down a full hour earlier than usual, and finds Mr. Henry Egerton in the breakfast-room, fresh from a night's travelling—(not, however, in his night-clothes)—bursting with all the longing impatience natural to his situation!

The rest of the family appeared to have come down unusually early this morning, and yet, on glancing at the clock, Blanche was obliged to confess that if anything it was the other way. And so that delicious *tête-à-tête* perforce came to an end. Harry stayed to receive the congratulations of the family over his breakfast, and then sallied forth again to Lincoln's Inn.

Calling at the club, he came in for more congratulations (sown by Villars the day before), and picked up one or two letters which he proceeded to open carelessly, as he answered that it didn't do to holloa before you were out of the wood—his little business was not yet settled.

One of his letters had been forwarded from Eaton Place, and had been lying at the club since the day he left for Ireland. The superscription savouring rather of the distressed tradesman, it was reserved for some minutes, and when opened at last the contents at first appeared to agree with the expectations suggested by the exterior of the envelope.

The writer began by saying that he had called in the hope of finding Mr. Henry Egerton at his father's house, but had failed both in that and in his attempt to find out his address.

Harry chuckled a little at his discomfiture, and looked on to the end, to see who the applicant was. The name was unknown to him,—and a surgeon in St. George's Hospital, too;—what might this mean? he wondered, as he continued with more interest than before.

There was, said his correspondent, at the time he wrote, a woman under his care, who had not many days to live, and who had repeatedly expressed a wish to see him, in order, he believed, to communicate some intelligence of importance, which seemed to be weighing upon her mind. If he desired to see her alive, he should repair to the hospital immediately on the receipt of this letter, and inquire for the writer, who had addressed to him in Eaton Place, on the chance of its ultimately reaching him from thence.

"Too late, I'm afraid," thought Harry, as he looked at the date; but he lost no time, notwithstanding, in calling a cab and directing the driver to St. George's Hospital. Curious, he thought, how everything seemed to be turning up in his favour; for of course this must be the woman who was missing. But why send for him instead of Philip? St. George's Hospital! This, then, was the reason why Frank Egerton had seen no more of her.

Further speculation was interrupted by his

arrival at the door. The surgeon was inquired for. He was shown into a private room; and a few moments after, enter to him his correspondent, who regretted that his letter had not reached its destination sooner, for the woman referred to was already buried. However, he believed that he had done all that it was possible to do under the circumstances, and after a few moments' absence from the room, he returned with a copy of a declaration which Rose M'Pherson had made before her death in presence of competent witnesses. It contained a confirmation of the statement which she had formerly sworn to in respect of Philip Egerton's parentage, and together with particulars which the surgeon could add, afforded satisfactory reasons for her claim not having been advanced before.

Dismissed from Castle Greville for dishonesty, her husband had been unable to find another place before their funds were all exhausted. They had come over to England,—her husband had died,—she had taken to begging, thieving, drinking,—had been concerned at last in criminal proceedings of a graver nature, convicted, sentenced for a long term of years, returned, convicted again, and on her release the second time had set herself to work to find out the condition of her son,—had even gone down on foot to Mr. Egerton's old place, which had been sold many years before, and had come back without hearing anything of the present residence of the family: the name was a common one, the places in their possession numerous. Not knowing whether the nurse was still alive, she had not risked a letter which, if opened, might spoil her chance of making the secret profitable. It was not easy for a ragged woman of her appearance to find out the particulars regarding anybody or anything; people were not in the habit of paying much attention to persons of her class; and she was beginning to despair of success, when her story, which was wont to be treated as a sort of hallucination by her associates, to whom she bragged of her son's position, came by chance to the ears of Flint the attorney.

Foreseeing a probability of gain, either from the elder son, who would pay to be confirmed in possession, or from the younger, who would pay for a proof of his right, the attorney induced her to make the affidavit, which he had copied,—had advertised as we have seen, and, only for his sudden death, had matters in train for bringing mother and son together once more. By his death she had been thrown back to where she was before; and as he had carefully concealed from her how far he had advanced in the matter, she had again given up hope, until it was unexpectedly revived by overhearing the conversation between Harry Egerton and his cousin. For some days she had watched in vain for Philip's coming out of his father's house. Philip was then at Aldershott. At last, the Saturday before his father's death, she had seen him leave the door. She knew Harry did not live there, it could only be her son—instinctively she knew that it was her son. But it was not until the following Monday, when she had watched Harry come and go from the house, that an opportunity of accosting Philip had occurred,—the results of that interview we know. For days she had lingered on unable to explain the cause of her accident. And when at last she recovered articulate speech, and was made aware that she had not long to live, her eagerness to see the man whom her heartless son was defrauding made such an impression upon the surgeon who attended her (who had had some slight acquaintance with Mr. Egerton years ago), that he had called himself in Eaton Place, and subsequently written the letter which originated the present interview. Harry was profuse in his acknowledgments of the obligations under which he lay, explaining to the surgeon how very opportunely his letter had arrived.

The other was glad to have been of any service in the cause of justice, hoped that Harry would command him in any way, and returned to his duties with the satisfaction of having contributed his mite to the rectification of wrong.

Egerton, meanwhile, more exhilarated than ever in his mind, posted off to Lincoln's Inn, laid his whole case, as now developed, before Mr. Naylor Bond, and asked him what he thought of it.

After listening attentively to the recital, the lawyer was fain to confess that it was now a strong one. The declaration, he said, could not be received in evidence in a civil case—but the surgeon would be a useful witness. He complimented him upon his promptitude in going himself to Ireland—wondered that he had not seen the so-called Mr. Philip Egerton the day before—believed that he would not give up possession easily, if he might judge from the state of his feelings on the last occasion when he had had the pleasure of seeing him; but had no doubt that Harry, with all this accumulation of evidence, would eventually triumph.

Harry returned to Grosvenor Square—as under such exciting circumstances he might be expected to return—in a cab.

CHAPTER XXI.

The interest of the world, the fashionable world more particularly, is not often solicited for two romances at once, as it was in this present year of grace in which our story lies. No sooner had the announcement of a Lord Belvedere having suddenly turned up gone the round of the papers, and been thoroughly discussed at every five-o'clock tea and morning call—no sooner had the interest excited by this out-of-the-way episode of the season calmed down, than another romance starts up, Phœnix-like, from its ashes.

Harry Egerton is now the talk of the town. Having been many seasons in London, he was pretty well known in general society. His father had been a well-known man; and Philip, from holding a commission in Her Majesty's Guards, was also known to a certain number of men. (It ought to be mentioned, for fear Philip should be a shock to the popular notion of the "Guardsman," that all Guardsmen do not by any means come up to the splendid ideals which figure so advantageously in novels. They are not all gay, dashing, handsome Lotharios. Many are ordinary young men enough—more than ordinary, some of them—and some few, I dare say, would find a much more congenial society at Aldershott.) However, this second claim upon the romantic sympathies of society was now in the height of its influence. Harry found himself a little lion in his way, and was perpetually receiving slaps on the back from good-natured friends, who wished him joy of his luck, and promised to come and stay with him in the winter. Blanche, too, was an object of much interest to ladies, young and old, for having had her constancy rewarded in so romantic a manner. Lady Belvedere even spared a thought or two from her own newly-aroused maternal interest, and told Harry that he didn't deserve such luck, after throwing over her plans for his marriage with her heiress. As for Miss Grant, she congratulated him with a very cold sincerity on the accession to independence which seemed in store for him, and added another figure to the gallery of gay deceivers through which it would be her delight to wander in the twilight of her spinsterhood, congratulating herself upon her escape. Lady Emily L'Estrange actually gave him her whole hand when next they met, and regretted that she had not done so before, when she considered how attentive he had been to Florence during the period of his poverty. The world generally, indeed, smiled upon him now. But however pleasant it might be to hear nothing but good wishes on all sides, Harry was painfully conscious that he was not yet in possession.

Philip had no notion of giving up what he held without a struggle. He had announced his intention of dying hard; congratulated himself that Harry had shown his hand; and was now leaving no stone unturned which might help in any way to break down the evidence arrayed against him.

Naylor Bond being inevitably engaged in Philip's interest, Harry had placed himself in the hands of Mr. Villars' solicitor, and under his instructions had brought an action of ejectment against his pseudo-brother for the coming assizes in August, the intervening period being devoted to the collection of such further evidence as might contribute to the strengthening of his case.

Time wore on; the season came to a close; the Villarses went to Homburg, and left him chafing at the suspense and delay in London. One by one the world dropped off. Maud Farringford had gone to Scotland, and taken her mother with her, to brace up her nerves for the coming trial. Manners had tantalised him with the offer of a berth again in his yacht; and Charlie had gone to Scotland too, after taking a cordial leave of him, and expressing the heartiest wishes for his success and speedy marriage. So he was left almost alone with his solicitor and his anxiety.

Quid multa? The day arrived at last; the judges have taken their seats; the jury are in their places; eminent counsel are ranged on either side (for once, Philip had not been chary of expense); the court is crowded; and the case comes on.

Again, *Quid multa?*

It was in vain that the learned gentlemen tried to discredit the Irishwoman's testimony by attempting to prove her mad. Since her mind had been relieved by a full confession, she seemed to have put on another nature; and the clearness and connectedness of her evidence belied the imbecility which they were attempting to prove. It was in vain that Mrs. Greville did her best to prejudice the case by losing her head and contradicting herself over and over again. It was in vain that they attempted to prove discrepancies between the woman M'Pherson's affidavit, Frank Egerton's story, and the surgeon's account of her dying revelations. It was in vain that every legal artifice and art was employed to obtain a verdict for the defendant; the case against them was too strong. The mass of circumstantial evidence which had been collected to back up the more substantial points of Harry's suit was too overpowering for the ingenuity of even those eminent lawyers; and the verdict was given in favour of the petitioner.

With what a thrill Harry received the intelligence! A telegram was at once despatched to Homburg; and for an hour or so he enjoyed much the same feelings as Lamb assigns to the gentleman who thought he had drawn a twenty-thousand-pound prize in the lottery. At the end of the hour, though, his feelings suffered the same reaction which this disappointed gentleman experienced on finding that, by a mistake of the clerk, a figure had been left out which reduced his twenty thousand pounds to a blank. Philip had announced his intention of appealing!

That dreadful word "appeal." What a long vista of interminable law did it suggest! and what a lean, well-picked figure was that at the end of it! What a sudden fall it produced in the barometer of Harry's spirits, as he thought that this would effectually put an end to all prospect of marriage for months to come. The hard, dry lawyer who communicated the fact of Philip's dogged resolution was almost moved by the dismayed and dismal look which his face assumed when he received the news.

Happily, however, for the exigencies of a final chapter, Philip was persuaded to forego his determination. His lawyers represented to him how futile it was to hope that he could ever obtain a verdict; how Harry must eventually triumph, and how Philip would only be exasperating him by involving him in a tedious lawsuit,—how much more for his interest it would be to accept the verdict with a good grace, and trust to his former brother's generosity, instead of hardening his heart against him by repeated appeals.

Philip was fully alive to the justice of their representations; and, though he would have dearly liked to keep Harry out as long as ever it was in his power to keep himself in, yet he knew that in the end he should be a beggar; and that, too, with very much less claim upon Harry's kindness than he could put forward now.

The latter, therefore, to his extreme delight, received a letter that very evening from Philip, couched in magnanimous terms, dwelling upon the forbearance which he was showing in not involving him in further expense, reminding him of all he (Philip) had intended to do for him, when he thought he was his brother, and winding up by some abject expressions of fawning servility, meanness, and deceit.

"Poor devil!" Harry exclaimed, as he put down the letter. "It *is* rather a come down,—and he might have given me a lot of trouble, if he had chosen. I dare say, though, he knew pretty well it wouldn't pay in the end."

The result of Philip's well-timed magnanimity was, that Harry made over to him the twenty thousand pounds, of which the very touch ought to have burned his fingers, and accompanied the gift with a generous letter, saying that although they were no longer brothers, there was no reason why they should not now be friends.

Philip, however, did not care about the friendship of a man who had ousted him from so much promised enjoyment; sold his commission, regretted by not a single man in his regiment; pocketed the proceeds, together with Harry's generous gift; and disappeared shortly after from the scene.

Frank Egerton was comfortably settled in the position of a gentleman for the remainder of his worn-out life. Accounts were gone into; creditors innumerable were disposed of; a mass of business transacted with Mr. Naylor Bond; settlements put in hand; and when all these matters had been arranged,— to Hancock's, and then, at last, to Homburg.

CHAPTER XXII.

Young ladies at least will admit the last scene to be important enough to have a chapter, however short, absolutely to itself.

The curtain, then, rises for the last time upon a bright November morning, a village church, evergreens, rustics in their Sunday best, homely faces, excited school-children, carriages, favoured footmen, red cloth, bright dresses, tripping bridesmaids, smart young men, gay old beaux, pealing bells, smiles, joy, gladness, enthusiasm everywhere.

Amid ringing cheers, and waving handkerchiefs and hats, and even tearful eyes, Blanche Egerton is issuing from the church upon her husband's arm. The crowd press back, and you recognise that blushing face, more softly beautiful than ever in her bridal white. You recognise, too, that late younger son who looks with such pride and tenderness on the true woman by his side. And if you have felt in them a tithe of the interest which they were intended to create, you wish them all the happiness and domestic bliss which one of them at least deserves.

Hey! presto! the scene is once more changed. Breakfast, dull speeches, all is over. The hall-door is thronged with friends waving their last adieux; the windows above are studded with servants' heads; the postillions crack their whips; the traditional slipper speeds upon its awkward flight after the departing carriage; and Harry Egerton and his bride are on their way to Leicestershire.

Heaven smiles upon their union; the great sun warms the air for them as they pass; little birds peep in at the windows, and fly on with a pleasant, sympathising chirp; the old trees shed their leaves in sorrow behind them; the rabbits take a last fond look at their young mistress from out those patches of brown fern; the deer gather round the gate to say farewell; and all the cottagers from their doors repeat the same, as the carriage dashes down the village row.

A night of storm has been succeeded by a day of soft, sunshiny calm; the drama is played out! *Valete, plaudite!*

THE END.

www.ingramcontent.com/pod-product-compliance
Lightning Source LLC
Chambersburg PA
CBHW032059220426
43664CB00008B/1059